THE INTERNATIONAL
PSYCHO-ANALYTICAL
LIBRARY
No. 4.

THE INTERNATIONAL PSYCHO-ANALYTICAL LIBRARY
EDITED BY ERNEST JONES, M.D.

No. 4

BEYOND
THE PLEASURE
PRINCIPLE

Sigmund Freud

A NEW TRANSLATION BY
JAMES STRACHEY

LIVERIGHT PUBLISHING CORPORATION
NEW YORK
1950

First published in German
under the title of Jenseits des Lustprinzips 1920
First published in English in 1922
Second Impression 1942
Third Impression 1948
This New Translation 1950

PRINTED IN GREAT BRITAIN
William Brown & Co. Ltd., London, E.C.3

TRANSLATOR'S NOTE

Jenseits des Lustprinzips was first published in 1920 by the Internationaler Psychoanalytischer Verlag (Leipzig, Vienna and Zurich). A second edition, with some changes and additions, appeared in 1921 and a third in 1923. The work was included in Volume VI of Freud's *Gesammelte Schriften* (issued by the same publishers) in 1925, and in Volume XIII of Freud's *Gesammelte Werke* (Imago Publishing Co., London) in 1940. An English translation by C. J. M. Hubback appeared in the International Psycho-Analytical Library in 1922.

The present, entirely new, version is based on the German text given in the *Gesammelte Werke*, but all substantial variants between this and the earlier editions have been indicated. Full details of works quoted in the text will be found in a list at the end of the volume. The responsibility for all material printed between square brackets is mine.

My thanks are due to Miss Anna Freud and Professor L. S. Penrose for reading through a draft of the translation and making a number of valuable suggestions.

J.S.

BEYOND THE PLEASURE PRINCIPLE

I

In the theory of psycho-analysis we have no hesitation in assuming that the course taken by mental events is automatically regulated by the pleasure principle. We believe, that is to say, that the course of those events is invariably set in motion by an unpleasurable tension, and that it takes a direction such that its final outcome coincides with a lowering of that tension—that is, with an avoidance of unpleasure or a production of pleasure. In taking that course into account in our consideration of the mental processes which are the subject of our study, we are introducing an 'economic' point of view into our work ; and if, in describing those processes, we try to estimate this 'economic' factor in addition to the 'topographical' and 'dynamic' ones, we shall, I think, be giving the most complete description of them of which we can at present conceive, and one which deserves to be distinguished by the term 'metapsychological.'

It is of no concern to us in this connection to enquire how far, with this hypothesis of the pleasure principle, we have approached or adopted any particular, historically established, philosophical system. We have arrived at these speculative assumptions in an attempt to describe and to account for the facts of daily observation in our field of study. Priority and originality are not among the aims that psycho-analytic work sets itself ; and the impressions that underlie the hypothesis of the pleasure principle are so obvious that they can scarcely be overlooked. On the other hand we would readily express our gratitude to any philosophical or psychological theory which was able to inform us of the meaning of the feelings of pleasure and unpleasure which act so imperatively upon us. But on this point we are, alas, offered nothing to our purpose. This is the most obscure and inaccessible region of the mind, and, since we cannot avoid contact with it, the least rigid hypothesis, it seems to me, will be the best. We have decided to relate pleasure and unpleasure to the quantity of excitation that is present in the mind but is not in any way ' bound ' ; and to relate them in such a manner that unpleasure corresponds to an *increase* in the quantity of excitation and pleasure to a *diminution*. What we are implying by this is not a simple relation between the strength of the feelings of pleasure and unpleasure and the corresponding modifications in the quantity of excitation ; least of all—in view of all we have been taught by psychophysiology—are we suggesting any directly proportional ratio : the factor that determines the feeling is probably the amount of increase or diminution in the quantity of excitation *in a given period of time*. Experiment might possibly play a part here ; but it is not advisable for us analysts to go into the problem further so long as our way is not pointed by quite definite observations.

We cannot however remain indifferent to the discovery that an investigator of such penetration as G. T. Fechner held a view upon the subject of pleasure and unpleasure which coincides in all essentials with the one that has been forced upon us by psycho-analytic work. Fechner's statement is to be found contained in a small work, *Einige Ideen zur Schöpfungs — und Entwicklungsgeschichte der Organismen*, 1873 (Part XI, Supplement, 94), and reads as follows : ' In so far as conscious impulses always have some relation to pleasure or unpleasure, pleasure and unpleasure too can be regarded as having a psycho-physical relation to conditions of stability and instability. This provides a basis for a hypothesis into which I propose to enter in greater detail elsewhere. According to this hypothesis, every psycho-physical movement crossing the threshold of consciousness is attended by pleasure in proportion as, beyond a certain limit, it approximates to complete stability, and is attended by unpleasure in proportion as, beyond a certain limit, it deviates from complete stability ; while between the two limits, which may be described as qualitative thresholds of pleasure and unpleasure, there is a certain margin of aesthetic indifference . . . . . '

The facts which have caused us to believe in the dominance of the pleasure principle in mental life also find expression in the hypothesis that the mental

3

apparatus endeavours to keep the quantity of excitation present in it as low as possible or at least to keep it constant. This latter hypothesis is only another way of stating the pleasure principle ; for if the work of the mental apparatus is directed towards keeping the quantity of excitation low, then anything that is calculated to increase that quantity is bound to be felt as adverse to the functioning of the apparatus, that is, as unpleasurable. The pleasure principle follows from the constancy principle : actually the constancy principle was inferred from the facts which forced us to adopt the pleasure principle.[1] Moreoever, a more detailed discussion will show that the tendency which we thus attribute to the mental apparatus is subsumed as a special case under Fechner's principle of the ' tendency towards stability,' to which he has brought the feelings of pleasure and unpleasure into relation.

It must be pointed out, however, that strictly speaking it is incorrect to talk of the dominance of the pleasure principle over the course of mental processes. If such a dominance existed, the immense majority of our mental processes would have to be

---

[1][The ' constancy principle ' dates back to the very beginning of Freud's psychological studies. It was first discussed at length by Breuer (in semi-physiological terms) in his theoretical section of the *Studies upon Hysteria* (Breuer and Freud, 1895, 171 ff). He there defines it as ' the tendency to maintain intra-cerebral excitation at a constant level.' In the same passage he attributes this principle to Freud and there in fact exist one or two earlier very brief references to it by Freud himself, though these were not published until after his death. (See Freud, 1892 and Breuer and Freud, 1892).]

accompanied by pleasure or to lead to pleasure, whereas universal experience completely contradicts any such conclusion. The most that can be said, therefore, is that there exists in the mind a strong *tendency* towards the pleasure principle, but that that tendency is opposed by certain other forces or circumstances, so that the final outcome cannot always be in harmony with the tendency towards pleasure. We may compare what Fechner (1873, 90) remarks on a similar point : ' Since however a tendency towards an aim does not imply that the aim is attained, and since in general the aim is attainable only by approximations . . . . .'

If we turn now to the question of what circumstances are able to prevent the pleasure principle from being carried into effect, we find ourselves once more on secure and well-trodden ground and, in framing our answer, we have at our disposal a rich fund of analytic experience.

The first example of the pleasure principle being inhibited in this way is a familiar one which occurs with regularity. We know that the pleasure principle is proper to a *primary* method of working on the part of the mental apparatus, but that, from the point of view of the self-preservation of the organism among the difficulties of the external world, it is from the very outset inefficient and even highly dangerous. Under the influence of the ego's instincts of self-preservation, the pleasure principle is replaced by the *reality principle*. This latter principle does not abandon the intention of ultimately obtaining pleasure, but it nevertheless demands and carries into effect the postponement of satisfaction, the abandonment of a number of possibilities of gaining satisfaction and the temporary toleration of unpleasure as a step on the long indirect road to pleasure. The pleasure principle long persists, however, as the method of working employed by the sexual instincts, which are so hard to ' educate,' and, starting out from those instincts, or in the ego itself, it often succeeds in overcoming the reality principle, to the detriment of the organism as a whole.

There can be no doubt, however, that the replacement of the pleasure principle by the reality principle can only be made responsible for a small number and by no means the most intense of unpleasurable experiences. Another occasion of the release of unpleasure, which occurs with no less regularity, is to be found in the conflicts and dissensions that take place in the mental apparatus while the ego is passing through its development into more highly composite organizations. Almost all the energy with which the apparatus is filled arises from its innate instinctual impulses, but these are not all allowed to reach the same phases of development. In the course of development it happens again and again that individual instincts or parts of instincts turn out to be incompatible in their aims or demands with the remaining ones, which are able to combine into the inclusive unity of the ego. The former are then split off from this unity by the process of repression, held back at lower levels of psychical development and cut off, to begin with, from the possibility of satisfaction. If they succeed subsequently, as can so easily happen with repressed sexual instincts, in struggling through, by roundabout paths, to a direct or to a substitutive satisfaction, that event, which would in other cases have been an opportunity for pleasure, is felt by the ego as unpleasure. As a consequence of the old conflict which ended in repression, a new breach has occurred in the pleasure principle at the very time when certain instincts were endeavouring, in accordance with the principle, to obtain fresh pleasure. The details of the process by which repression turns a possibility of pleasure into a source of unpleasure are not yet clearly understood or cannot be clearly represented ; but there is no doubt that all neurotic unpleasure is of that kind—pleasure that cannot be felt as such.

The two sources of unpleasure which I have just indicated are very far from covering the majority of our unpleasurable experiences. But as regards the remainder it can be asserted with some show of justification that their presence does not contradict the dominance of the pleasure principle. Most of the unpleasure that we experience is *perceptual* unpleasure : either perception of pressure by unsatisfied instincts, or external perception which is either distressing in itself or which excites unpleasurable expectations in the mental apparatus, that is,

---

[2][Footnote added 1925 :] No doubt the essential point is that pleasure and unpleasure, being conscious feelings, are attached to the ego.

which is recognized by it as a ' danger.' The reaction to these instinctual demands and threats of danger, a reaction which constitutes the proper activity of the mental apparatus, can then be directed in a correct manner by the pleasure principle or the modified reality principle. This does not seem to necessitate any far-reaching limitation of the pleasure principle. Nevertheless the investigation of the mental reaction to external danger is precisely a subject which may produce new material and raise fresh questions bearing upon our present problem.

II

A condition has long been known and described which occurs after severe mechanical concussions, railway disasters and other accidents involving a risk to life ; it has been given the name of ' traumatic neurosis.' The terrible war which has just ended gave rise to a great number of illnesses of this kind, but it at least put an end to the temptation to attribute the cause of the disorder to organic lesions of the nervous system brought about by mechanical force.[3] The symptomatic picture presented by traumatic neurosis approaches that of hysteria in the wealth of its similar motor symptoms, but surpasses it as a rule in its strongly marked signs of subjective ailment (in which it resembles hypochondria or melancholia) as well as in the evidence it gives of a far more comprehensive general enfeeblement and disturbance of the mental capacities. No complete explanation has yet been reached either of war neuroses or of the traumatic neuroses of peace. In the case of the war neuroses, the fact that the same symptoms sometimes came about without the intervention of any gross mechanical violence seemed at once enlightening and bewildering. In the case of the ordinary traumatic neuroses two characteristics

[3]Cf. the discussion on the psycho-analysis of the war neuroses by Freud, Ferenczi, Abraham, Simmel and Jones (1919).

emerge prominently : first, that the chief weight in their causation seems to rest upon the factor of surprise, of fright ; and secondly that a wound or injury inflicted simultaneously works as a rule *against* the development of a neurosis. ' Fright,' ' fear ' and ' anxiety '[4] are improperly used as synonymous expressions ; they are in fact capable of clear distinction in their relation to danger. ' Anxiety ' describes a particular state of expecting the danger or preparing for it, even though it may be an unknown one. ' Fear ' requires a definite object of which to be afraid. ' Fright,' however, is the name we give to the state a person gets into when he has run into danger without being prepared for it ; it emphasizes the factor of surprise. I do not believe anxiety can produce a traumatic neurosis. There is something about anxiety that protects its subject against fright and so against fright-neuroses. We shall return to this point later. [See page 38 f.]

The study of dreams may be considered the most trustworthy method of investigating deep mental processes. Now dreams occurring in traumatic neuroses have the characteristic of repeatedly bringing the patient back into the situation of his accident, a situation from which he wakes up in another fright. This astonishes people far too little. They think the fact that the traumatic experience is constantly forcing itself upon the patient even in his sleep is a proof of the strength of that experience : the patient is, as one might say, fixated to his trauma.

[4] [In German, ' *Schreck*,' ' *Furcht* ' and ' *Angst*.']

Fixations to the experience which started the illness have long been familiar to us in hysteria. Breuer and Freud declared in 1893 that hysterics are to a great extent suffering from reminiscences. In the war neuroses, too, observers like Ferenczi and Simmel have been able to explain certain motor symptoms by fixation to the moment at which the trauma occurred.

I am not aware, however, that patients suffering from traumatic neurosis are much occupied in their waking lives with memories of their accident. Perhaps they are more concerned with *not* thinking of it. Anyone who accepts it as something self-evident that their dreams should put them back at night into the situation that caused them to fall ill has misunderstood the nature of dreams. It would be more in harmony with their nature to show the patient pictures from his healthy past or of the cure for which he hopes. If we are not to be shaken in our belief in the wish-fulfilling tenor of dreams by the dreams of traumatic neurotics, we still have one resource open to us : we may argue that the function of dreaming, like so much else, is upset in this condition and diverted from its purposes, or we may be driven to reflect on the mysterious masochistic trends of the ego.[5]

At this point I propose to leave the dark and dismal subject of the traumatic neurosis and pass on to examine the method of working employed by

---

[5][The last clause of this sentence was added in 1921.]

the mental apparatus in one of its earliest *normal* activities—I mean in children's play.

The different theories of children's play have only recently been summarized and discussed from the psycho-analytic point of view by Pfeifer (1919), to whose paper I would refer my readers. These theories attempt to discover the motives which lead children to play, but they fail to bring into the foreground the *economic* motive, the consideration of the yield of pleasure involved. Without wishing to include the whole field covered by these phenomena, I have been able, through a chance opportunity which presented itself, to throw some light upon the first game played by a little boy of one and a half and invented by himself. It was more than a mere fleeting observation, for I lived under the same roof as the child and his parents for some weeks, and it was some time before I discovered the meaning of the puzzling activity which he constantly repeated.

The child was not at all precocious in his intellectual development. At the age of one and a half he could say only a few comprehensible words ; he could also make use of a number of sounds which expressed a meaning intelligible to those around him. He was, however, on good terms with his parents and their one servant-girl, and tributes were paid to his being a ' good boy.' He did not disturb his parents at night, he conscientiously obeyed orders not to touch certain things or go into certain rooms, and above all he never cried when his mother left him for a few hours. At the same time, he was greatly attached to his mother, who had not only fed him herself but had also looked after him without any outside help. This good little boy, however, had an occasional disturbing habit of taking any small objects he could get hold of and throwing them away from him into a corner, under the bed, and so on, so that hunting for his toys and picking them up was often quite a business. As he did this he gave vent to a loud, long-drawn-out ' o-o-o-o,' accompanied by an expression of interest and satisfaction. His mother and the writer of the present account were agreed in thinking that this was not a mere interjection but represented the German word '*fort*' ['gone']. I eventually realized that it was a game and that the only use he made of any of his toys was to play 'gone' with them. One day I made an observation which confirmed my view. The child had a wooden reel with a piece of string tied round it. It never occurred to him to pull it along the floor behind him, for instance, and play at its being a carriage. What he did was to hold the reel by the string and very skilfully throw it over the edge of his curtained cot, so that it disappeared into it, at the same time uttering his expressive ' o-o-o-o.' He then pulled the reel out of the cot again by the string and hailed its reappearance with a joyful ' *da* ' ['there']. This, then, was the complete game—disappearance and return. As a rule one only witnessed its first act, which was repeated untiringly as a game in itself, though there is no doubt that greater pleasure was attached to the second act.[6]

The interpretation of the game then became obvious. It was related to the child's great cultural achievement—the instinctual renunciation (that is, the renunciation of instinctual satisfaction) which he had made in allowing his mother to go away without protesting. He compensated himself for this, as it were, by himself staging the disappearance and return of the objects within his reach. It is of course a matter of indifference from the point of view of judging the affective nature of the game whether the child invented it himself or took it over on some outside suggestion. Our interest is directed to another point. The child cannot possibly have felt his mother's departure as something agreeable or even indifferent. How then does his repetition of this distressing experience as a game fit in with the pleasure principle? It may perhaps be said in reply that her departure had to be enacted as a necessary preliminary to her joyful return, and that it was in the latter that lay the true purpose of the game. But against this must be counted the observed

---

[6] A further observation subsequently confirmed this interpretation fully. One day the child's mother had been away for several hours and on her return was met with the words ' Baby o-o-o-o ! ' which was at first incomprehensible. It soon turned out, however, that during this long period of solitude the child had found a method of making *himself* disappear. He had discovered his reflection in a full-length mirror which did not quite reach to the ground, so that by crouching down he could make his mirror-image ' gone.'

fact that the first act, that of the departure, was staged as a game in itself and far more frequently than the episode in its entirety with its pleasurable ending.

No certain decision can be reached from the analysis of a single case like this. On an unprejudiced view one gets an impression that the child turned his experience into a game from another motive. At the outset he was in a *passive* situation—he was overpowered by the experience ; but, by repeating it, unpleasurable though it was, as a game, he took on an *active* part. These efforts might be put down to an instinct for mastery acting independently of whether the [repeated] memory were in itself pleasurable or not. But still another interpretation may be attempted. Throwing away the object so that it was ' gone ' might satisfy an impulse of the child's, which was suppressed in his actual life, to revenge himself on his mother for going away from him. In that case it would have a defiant meaning : ' All right, then, go away ! I don't need you. I'm sending you away myself.' A year later, the same boy whom I had observed at his first game used to take a toy, if he was angry with it, and throw it on the floor, exclaiming : ' Go to the fwont ! ' He had heard at that time that his absent father was ' at the front,' and was far from regretting his absence ; on the contrary he made it quite clear that he had no desire to be disturbed in his sole possession of his mother.[7] We know of other children who liked to

---

[7] When this child was five and three-quarters, his mother died. Now that she was really ' gone ' (' o-o-o '), the little boy showed no signs of grief. It is true that in the interval a second child had been born and had roused him to violent jealousy.

express similar hostile impulses by throwing away objects instead of persons. (Cf. Freud, 1917). We are therefore left in doubt as to whether the impulse to work over in the mind some overpowering experience so as to make oneself master of it can find expression as a primary event, and independently of the pleasure principle. For, in the case we have been discussing, the child may, after all, only have been able to repeat his unpleasant experience in play because the repetition carried along with it a yield of pleasure of another sort but none the less a direct one.

Nor shall we be helped in our hesitation between these two views by further considering children's play. It is clear that in their play children repeat everything that has made a great impression on them in real life, and that in so doing they abreact the strength of the impression and, as one might put it, make themselves master of the situation. But on the other hand it is obvious that all their play is influenced by a wish that dominates them the whole time—the wish to be grown-up and to be able to do what grown-up people do. It can also be observed that the unpleasurable nature of an experience does not always unsuit it for play. If the doctor looks down a child's throat or carries out some small operation on him, we may be quite sure that these frightening experiences will be the subject of the next game ; but we must not in that connection overlook the fact that there is a yield of pleasure from another source. As the child passes over from the passivity of the experience to the activity of the game, he hands on the disagreeable experience to one of his playmates and in this way revenges himself on a substitute.

Nevertheless, it emerges from this discussion that there is no need to assume the existence of a special imitative instinct in order to provide a motive for play. Finally, a reminder may be added that the artistic play and artistic imitation carried out by adults, which, unlike children's, are aimed at an audience, do not spare the spectators (in tragedy, for instance) the most painful experiences and can yet be felt by them as highly enjoyable. This is convincing proof that, even under the dominance of the pleasure principle, there are ways and means enough of making what is in itself unpleasurable into a subject to be recollected and worked over in the mind. The consideration of these cases and situations, which have a yield of pleasure as their final outcome, should be undertaken by some system of aesthetics with an economic approach to its subject-matter. They are of no use for *our* purposes, since they presuppose the existence and dominance of the pleasure principle ; they give no evidence of the operation of tendencies *beyond* the pleasure principle, that is, of tendencies more primitive than it and independent of it.

III

Twenty-five years of intense work have had as their result that the immediate aims of psycho-analytic technique are quite other to-day than they were at the outset. At first the analysing physician could do no more than discover the unconscious material that was concealed from the patient, put it together, and, at the right moment, communicate it to him. Psycho-analysis was then first and foremost an art of interpreting. Since this did not solve the therapeutic problem, a further aim quickly came in view : to oblige the patient to confirm the analyst's construction from his own memory. In that endeavour the chief emphasis lay upon the patient's resistances : the art consisted now in uncovering these as quickly as possible, in pointing them out to the patient and in inducing him by human influence—this was where suggestion operating as ' transference ' played its part—to abandon his resistances.

But it became ever clearer that the aim which had been set up—namely, that what was unconscious should become conscious—is not completely attainable by that method. The patient cannot remember the whole of what is repressed in him, and what he cannot remember may be precisely the essential part of it. Thus he acquires no sense of conviction of the correctness of the construction that has been communicated to him. He is obliged to *repeat* the repressed material as a contemporary experience instead of, as the physician would prefer to see, *remembering* it as something belonging to the past. (Cf. Freud, 1914*b*.) These reproductions, which emerge with such unwished-for exactitude, always have as their subject some portion of infantile sexual life—of the Oedipus complex, that is, and its derivatives ; and they are invariably played out in the sphere of the transference, of the patient's relation to the physician. When things have reached this stage, it may be said that the earlier neurosis has now been replaced by a fresh, ' transference neurosis.' It has been the physician's endeavour to keep this transference neurosis within the narrowest limits : to force as much as possible into the channel of memory and to allow as little as possible to emerge as repetition. The ratio between what is remembered and what is reproduced varies from case to case. The physician cannot as a rule spare his patient this phase of the treatment. He must get him to re-experience some portion of his forgotten life, but must see to it, on the other hand, that the patient retains some degree of aloofness, which will enable him, in spite of everything, to recognize that what appears to be reality is in fact only a reflection of a forgotten past. If this can be successfully achieved, the patient's sense of conviction is won, together with the therapeutic success that is dependent on it.

In order to make it easier to understand this ' compulsion to repeat,' which emerges during the psycho-analytic treatment of neurotics, we must above all get rid of the mistaken notion that what we are dealing with in our struggle against resistances is resistance on the part of the *unconscious*. The unconscious—that is to say, the ' repressed '—offers no resistance whatever to the efforts of the treatment. Indeed, it itself has no other endeavour than to break through the pressure weighing down on it and force its way either into consciousness or to discharge through some real action. Resistance during treatment arises from the same higher strata and systems of the mind which originally carried out repression. But the fact that, as we know from experience, the motives of the resistances, and indeed the resistances themselves, are unconscious at first during the treatment, is a hint to us that we should correct a shortcoming in our terminology. We shall avoid a lack of clarity if we make our contrast not between the conscious and the unconscious but between the coherent *ego* and the *repressed*. It is certain that much of the ego is itself unconscious, and notably what we may describe as its nucleus ; only a small part of it is covered by the term ' preconscious.'[8] Having replaced a purely descriptive terminology by one which is systematic or dynamic, we can say that the patient's resistance arises from his ego, and we then at once perceive that the compulsion to

---

[8][In its present form this sentence dates from 1921. In the first edition (1920) it ran : ' It may be that much of the ego is itself unconscious ; only a part of it, probably, is covered by the term " preconscious ".']

repeat must be ascribed to the unconscious repressed. It seems probable that that compulsion can only express itself after the work of treatment has gone half-way to meet it and has loosened the repression.[9]

There is no doubt that the resistance of the conscious and unconscious ego operates under the sway of the pleasure principle : it seeks to avoid the unpleasure which would be produced by the liberation of the repressed. Our efforts, on the other hand, are directed towards procuring the toleration of that unpleasure by an appeal to the reality principle. But how is the compulsion to repeat—the manifestation of the power of the repressed—related to the pleasure principle ? It is clear that the greater part of what is re-experienced under the compulsion to repeat must cause the ego unpleasure, since it brings to light activities of repressed instinctual impulses. That, however, is unpleasure of a kind we have already considered and does not contradict the pleasure principle : unpleasure for one system and simultaneously satisfaction for the other. But we come now to a new and remarkable fact, namely that the compulsion to repeat also recalls from the past experiences which include no possibility of pleasure, and which can never, even long ago, have brought satisfaction even to instinctual impulses which have since been repressed.

[9][Footnote added 1923 :] I have argued elsewhere [1923 ; English translation, 1950, 145] that what thus comes to the help of the compulsion to repeat is the factor of ' suggestion ' in the treatment—that is, the patient's submissiveness to the physician, which has its roots deep in his unconscious parental complex.

BEYOND THE PLEASURE PRINCIPLE

The early efflorescence of infantile sexual life is doomed to come to an end because its wishes are incompatible with reality and with the inadequate stage of development which the child has reached. That efflorescence perishes in the most distressing circumstances and to the accompaniment of the most painful feelings. Loss of love and failure leave behind them a permanent injury to self-assurance in the form of a narcissistic scar, which in my opinion, as well as in Marcinowski's (1918), contributes more than anything to the ' sense of inferiority ' which is so common in neurotics. Sexual researches, on which limits are imposed by a child's physical development, lead to no satisfactory conclusion ; hence such later complaints as ' I can't accomplish anything ; I can't succeed in anything.' The tie of affection, which binds the child as a rule to the parent of the opposite sex, succumbs to disappointment, to a vain expectation of satisfaction or to jealousy over the birth of a new baby—unmistakable proof of the infidelity of the object of the child's affections. His own attempt to make a baby himself, carried out with tragic seriousness, fails shamefully. The lessening amount of affection he receives, the increasing demands of education, hard words and an occasional punishment—these show him at last the full extent to which he has been scorned. These are a few typical and constantly recurring instances of the ways in which the love characteristic of the age of childhood is brought to an end.

Patients repeat all of these unwanted situations

and painful emotions in the transference and revive them with the greatest ingenuity. They seek to bring about the interruption of the treatment while it is still incomplete ; they contrive once more to feel themselves scorned, to oblige the physician to speak severely to them and treat them coldly ; they discover appropriate objects for their jealousy ; instead of the passionately desired baby of their childhood, they produce a plan or a promise of some grand present—which turns out as a rule to be no less unreal. None of these things can have produced pleasure in the past ; and it might be supposed that they would cause less unpleasure to-day if they emerged as memories or dreams rather than taking the form of fresh experiences. They are of course the activities of instincts intended to lead to satisfaction ; but no lesson has been learnt from the old experience of these activities having led instead only to unpleasure.[10] In spite of that they are repeated, under pressure of a compulsion.

What psycho-analysis reveals in the transference phenomena of neurotics can also be observed in the lives of some normal people. The impression they give is of being pursued by a malignant fate or possessed by some extraneous power ; but psycho-analysis has always taken the view that their fate is for the most part arranged by themselves and determined by early infantile influences. The compulsion which is here in evidence differs in no way from the compulsion to repeat which we have found

---

[10][This sentence was added in 1921.]

in neurotics, even though the people we are now considering have never shown any signs of dealing with a neurotic conflict by producing symptoms. Thus we have come across people all of whose human relationships have the same outcome : such as the benefactor who is abandoned in anger after a time by each of his *protégés*, however much they may otherwise differ from one another, and who thus seems doomed to taste all the bitterness of ingratitude ; or the man whose friendships all end in betrayal by his friend ; or the man who time after time in the course of his life raises someone else into a position of great private or public authority and then, after a certain interval, himself upsets that authority and replaces him by a new one ; or, again, the lover each of whose love affairs with a woman passes through the same phases and reaches the same conclusion. This ' *ewige Wiederkehr des Gleichen* '[11] causes us no astonishment when it relates to *active* behaviour on the part of the person concerned and when we can discern in him an essential character-trait which always remains the same and which is compelled to find expression in a repetition of the same experiences. We are much more impressed by cases where the subject appears to have a *passive* experience, over which he has no influence, but in which he meets with a repetition of the same fatality. There is the case, for instance, of the woman who married three successive husbands each of whom fell ill soon after-wards and had to be nursed by her on their death-

---

[11][This ' perpetual recurrence of the same thing.']

beds.[12] The most moving poetic picture of a fate such as this is given by Tasso in his romantic epic *Gerusalemme Liberata*. Its hero, Tancred, unwittingly kills his beloved Clorinda in a duel while she is disguised in the armour of an enemy knight. After her burial he makes his way into a strange magic forest which strikes the Crusaders' army with terror. He slashes with his sword at a tall tree ; but blood streams from the cut and the voice of Clorinda, whose soul is imprisoned in the tree, is heard complaining that he has wounded his beloved once again.

If we take into account observations such as these, based upon behaviour in the transference and upon the life-histories of men and women, we shall find courage to assume that there really does exist in the mind a compulsion to repeat which overrides the pleasure principle. Now too we shall be inclined to relate to this compulsion the dreams which occur in traumatic neuroses and the impulse which leads children to play. It is to be noted, however, that only in rare instances can we observe the pure effects of the compulsion to repeat, unsupported by other motives. In the case of children's play we have already laid stress on the other ways in which the emergence of the compulsion may be interpreted ; the compulsion to repeat and instinctual satisfaction which is immediately pleasurable seem to converge here into an intimate partnership. The phenomena of transference are obviously exploited by the resist-

---

[12]Cf. the apt remarks on this subject by C. G. Jung (1909). [English translation, 1916, 168 f.]

ance which the ego maintains in its pertinacious insistence upon repression ; the compulsion to repeat, which the treatment tries to bring into its service, is enticed over to its side,[13] as it were, by the ego, clinging as it does to the pleasure principle. A great deal of what might be described as the compulsion of destiny seems intelligible on a rational basis ; so that we are under no necessity to call in a new and mysterious motive to explain it. The least dubious instance [of the presence of such a motive] is perhaps that of traumatic dreams ; but on maturer reflection we shall be forced to admit that even in the other instances the whole ground is not covered by the operation of the familiar motives. Enough is left unexplained to justify the hypothesis of a compulsion to repeat— something that seems more primitive, more elementary, more instinctual than the pleasure principle which it sets aside. But if a compulsion to repeat *does* operate in the mind, we should be glad to know something about it, to learn what function it corresponds to, under what conditions it can emerge and what its relation is to the pleasure principle—to which, after all, we have hitherto ascribed dominance over the course of the processes of excitation in mental life.

---

[13][Before 1923 this read ' is called to its help '.]

IV

What follows is speculation, often far-fetched speculation, which the reader will consider or dismiss according to his individual predilection. It is further an attempt to follow out an idea consistently, out of curiosity to see where it will lead.

Psycho-analytic speculation takes as its point of departure the impression, derived from examining unconscious processes, that consciousness may be, not the most universal attribute of mental processes, but only a particular function of them. Speaking in metapsychological terms, it asserts that consciousness is a function of a particular system which it describes as Cs.[14] What consciousness yields consists essentially of perceptions of excitations coming from the external world and of feelings of pleasure and unpleasure which can only arise from within the mental apparatus ; it is therefore possible to assign to the system Pcpt.-Cs.[15] a position in space. It must lie on the borderline between outside and inside ; it must be turned towards the external world and

---

[14][See Freud, 1900, Chapter VII, Section F, and Freud, 1915*b*, Section II (English translation, 1925,105).]

[15][The system Pcpt. (the perceptual system) was first described by Freud in Section B of Chapter VII of *The Interpretation of Dreams* (1900 ; English translation, 1932, 495 ff). In a later paper (Freud, 1916 ; English translation, 1925, 147) he showed that the system Pcpt. coincided with the system Cs.]

must envelop the other psychical systems. It will be seen that there is nothing daringly new in these assumptions ; we have merely adopted the views on localization held by cerebral anatomy, which locates the ' seat ' of consciousness in the cerebral cortex— the outermost, enveloping layer of the central organ. Cerebral anatomy has no need to consider why, speaking anatomically, consciousness should be lodged on the surface of the brain instead of being safely housed somewhere in its inmost interior. Perhaps *we* shall be more successful in accounting for this situation in the case of our system Pcpt.-Cs.

Consciousness is not the only distinctive character which we ascribe to the processes in that system. On the basis of impressions derived from our psycho-analytic experience, we assume that all excitatory processes that occur in the *other* systems leave permanent traces behind in them which form the foundation of memory. Such memory traces, then, have nothing to do with the fact of becoming conscious ; indeed they are often most powerful and most enduring when the process which left them behind was one which never entered consciousness. We find it hard to believe, however, that permanent traces of excitation such as these are also left in the system Pcpt.-Cs. If they remained constantly conscious, they would very soon set limits to the system's aptitude for receiving fresh excitations[16]. If, on the other

---

[16]What follows is based throughout on Breuer's discussion in the theoretical section of *Studien über Hysterie* (Breuer and Freud, 1895, [164 n.]).

hand, they were unconscious, we should be faced with the problem of explaining the existence of unconscious processes in a system whose functioning was otherwise accompanied by the phenomenon of consciousness. We should, so to say, have altered nothing and gained nothing by our hypothesis relegating the process of becoming conscious to a special system. Though this consideration is not absolutely conclusive, it nevertheless leads us to suspect that becoming conscious and leaving behind a memory trace are processes incompatible with each other within one and the same system. Thus we should be able to say that the excitatory process becomes conscious in the system Cs. but leaves no permanent trace behind there ; but that the excitation is transmitted to the systems lying next within and that it is in *them* that its traces are left. I followed these same lines in the schematic picture which I included in the speculative section of my *Interpretation of Dreams*.[17] It must be borne in mind that little enough is known from other sources of the origin of consciousness ; when, therefore, we lay down the proposition that consciousness arises instead of a memory trace,[18] the assertion deserves consideration, at all events on the ground of its being framed in fairly precise terms.

If this is so, then, the system Cs. is characterized by the peculiarity that in it (in contrast to what happens in the other psychical systems) excitatory

---

[17][Freud, 1900 ; English translation, 1932, 496.]
[18][The last six words are in spaced type in the original.]

processes do not leave behind any permanent change in its elements but expire, as it were, in the phenomenon of becoming conscious. An exception of this sort to the general rule requires to be explained by some factor that applies exclusively to that one system. Such a factor, which is absent in the other systems, might well be the exposed situation of the system Cs., immediately abutting as it does on the external world.

Let us picture a living organism in its most simplified possible form as an undifferentiated vesicle of a substance that is susceptible to stimulation. Then the surface turned towards the external world will from its very situation be differentiated and will serve as an organ for receiving stimuli. Indeed embryology, in its capacity as a recapitulation of developmental history, actually shows us that the central nervous system originates from the ectoderm ; the grey matter of the cortex remains a derivative of the primitive superficial layer of the organism and may have inherited some of its essential properties. It would be easy to suppose, then, that as a result of the ceaseless impact of external stimuli on the surface of the vesicle, its substance to a certain depth may have become permanently modified, so that excitatory processes run a different course in it from what they run in the deeper layers. A crust would thus be formed which would at last have been so thoroughly baked through by stimulation that it would present the most favourable possible conditions for the reception of stimuli and become

incapable of any further modification. In terms of
the system Cs., this would mean that its elements
could undergo no further permanent modification
from the passage of excitation, because they had
already been modified in the respect in question
to the greatest possible extent : now, however, they
would have become capable of giving rise to consciousness. Various ideas may be formed which cannot
at present be verified as to the nature of this modification of the substance and of the excitatory process.
It may be supposed that, in passing from one element
to another, an excitation has to overcome a resistance,
and that the diminution of resistance thus effected
is what lays down a permanent trace of the excitation,
that is, a pathway [*Bahnung*]. In the system Cs., then,
resistance of this kind to passage from one element to
another would no longer exist. This picture can be
brought into relation with Breuer's distinction between
quiescent (or 'bound') and mobile cathectic energy in
the elements of the psychical systems ;[19] the elements
of the system Cs. would carry no bound energy
but only energy capable of free discharge. It seems
best, however, to express oneself as cautiously as
possible on these points. None the less, this speculation
will have enabled us to bring the origin of consciousness into some sort of connection with the situation
of the system Cs. and with the peculiarities that
must be ascribed to the excitatory processes taking
place in it.

But we have more to say of the living vesicle

---

[19]Breuer and Freud, 1895 [167 ff].

with its receptive cortical layer. This little fragment of living substance is suspended in the middle of an external world charged with the most powerful energies ; and it would be killed by the stimulation emanating from these if it were not provided with a protective shield against stimuli. It acquires the shield in this way : its outermost surface ceases to have the structure proper to living matter, becomes to some degree inorganic and thenceforward functions as a special envelope or membrane resistant to stimuli. In consequence, the energies of the external world are able to pass into the next underlying layers, which have remained living, with only a fragment of their original intensity ; and these layers can devote themselves, behind the protective shield, to the reception of the amounts of stimulus which have been allowed through it. By its death, the outer layer has saved all the deeper ones from a similar fate—unless, that is to say, stimuli reach it which are so strong that they break through the protective shield. *Protection* against stimuli is an almost more important function for the living organism than *reception* of stimuli. The protective shield is supplied with its own store of energy and must above all endeavour to preserve the special forms of conversion of energy operating in it against the effects threatened by the enormous energies at work in the external world—effects which tend towards an equalization of potential and hence towards destruction. The main purpose of the *reception* of stimuli is to discover the direction and nature of the external stimuli ; and for that it is enough to take small specimens of the external world, to sample it in small quantities. In highly developed organisms the receptive cortical layer of the former vesicle has long been withdrawn into the depths of the interior of the body, though portions of it have been left behind on the surface immediately beneath the general shield against stimuli. These are the sense organs, which consist essentially of apparatus for the reception of certain specific effects of stimulation, but which also include special arrangements for further protection against excessive amounts of stimulation and for excluding unsuitable kinds of stimuli. It is characteristic of them that they deal only with very small quantities of external stimulation and only take in samples of the external world. They may perhaps be compared with feelers which are all the time making tentative advances towards the external world and then drawing back from it.

At this point I shall venture to touch for a moment upon a subject which would merit the most exhaustive treatment. As a result of certain psycho-analytic discoveries, we are to-day in a position to embark on a discussion of the Kantian theorem that time and space are ' necessary forms of thought.' We have learnt that unconscious mental processes are in themselves ' timeless '. This means in the first place that they are not ordered in time, that time does not change them in any way and that the idea of time cannot be applied to them. These are negative characteristics which can only be clearly understood if a comparison is made with *conscious* mental processes. On the other hand, our abstract idea of time seems to be wholly derived from the method of working of the system Pcpt.-Cs. and to correspond to a perception on its own part of that method of working. This mode of functioning may perhaps constitute another way of providing a shield against stimuli. I know that these remarks must sound very obscure, but I must limit myself to these hints.[20]

We have pointed out how the living vesicle is provided with a shield against stimuli from the external world ; and we had previously shown that the cortical layer next to that shield must be differentiated as an organ for receiving stimuli from without. This sensitive cortex, however, which is later to become the system Cs., also receives excitations from *within*. The situation of the system between the outside and the inside and the difference between the conditions governing the reception of excitations in the two cases have a decisive effect on the functioning of the system and of the whole mental apparatus. Towards the outside it is shielded against stimuli, and the amounts of excitation impinging on it have only a reduced effect. Towards the inside there can be no such shield ; the excitations in the deeper layers extend into the system directly and in undiminished amount, in so far as certain of their characteristics give rise to feelings in the pleasure-unpleasure series. The excitations coming from within are, however, in their intensity and in other, qualitative, respects—

---

[20][Freud later (1925) explained this point rather more fully.]

in their amplitude, perhaps—more commensurate with the system's method of working than the stimuli which stream in from the external world. This state of things produces two definite results. First, the feelings of pleasure and unpleasure (which are an index to what is happening in the interior of the apparatus) predominate over all external stimuli. And secondly, a particular way is adopted of dealing with any internal excitations which produce too great an increase of unpleasure : there is a tendency to treat them as though they were acting, not from the inside, but from the outside, so that it may be possible to bring the shield against stimuli into operation as a means of defence against them. This is the origin of *projection*, which is destined to play such a large part in the causation of pathological processes.

I have an impression that these last considerations have brought us to a better understanding of the dominance of the pleasure principle ; but no light has yet been thrown on the cases that contradict that dominance. Let us therefore go a step further. We describe as 'traumatic' any excitations from outside which are powerful enough to break through the protective shield. It seems to me that the concept of trauma necessarily implies a connection of this kind with a breach in an otherwise efficacious barrier against stimuli. Such an event as an external trauma is bound to provoke a disturbance on a large scale in the functioning of the organism's energy and to set in motion every possible defensive measure.

At the same time, the pleasure principle is for the moment put out of action. There is no longer any possibility of preventing the mental apparatus from being flooded with large amounts of stimulus, and another problem arises instead—the problem of mastering the amounts of stimulus which have broken in and of binding them, in the psychical sense, so that they can subsequently be discharged.

The specific unpleasure of physical pain is probably the result of the protective shield having been broken through in a limited area. There is then a continuous stream of excitations from the part of the periphery concerned to the central apparatus of the mind, such as could normally arise only from *within* the apparatus.[21] And how shall we expect the mind to react to this invasion ? Cathectic energy is summoned from all sides to provide sufficiently high cathexes of energy in the environs of the breach. An ' anticathexis ' on a grand scale is set up, for whose benefit all the other psychical systems are impoverished, so that the remaining psychical functions are extensively paralysed or reduced. We must endeavour to draw a lesson from examples such as this and use them as a basis for our metapsychological speculations. From the present case, then, we infer that a system which is itself highly cathected is capable of taking up an additional stream of fresh inflowing energy and of converting it into quiescent cathexis, that is of ' binding ' it psychically. The higher the system's own quiescent

---

[21]Cf. Freud, 1915a [English translation, 1925, 62].

cathexis, the greater seems to be its binding force ; conversely, therefore, the lower its cathexis, the less capacity will it have for taking up inflowing energy and the more violent must be the consequences of such a breach in the protective shield against stimuli. To this view it cannot be justly objected that the increase of cathexis round the breach can be explained far more simply as the direct result of the inflowing masses of excitation. If that were so, the mental apparatus would merely receive an increase in its cathexes of energy, and the paralysing character of pain and the impoverishment of all the other systems would remain unexplained. Nor do the very violent phenomena of discharge to which pain gives rise affect our explanation, for they occur in a reflex manner—that is, they follow without the intervention of the mental apparatus. The indefiniteness of all our discussions on what we describe as metapsychology is of course due to the fact that we know nothing of the nature of the excitatory process that takes place in the elements of the psychical systems, and that we do not feel justified in framing any hypothesis on the subject. We are consequently operating all the time with a large unknown quantity, which we are obliged to carry over into every new formula. It may be reasonably supposed that this excitatory process can be carried out with energies that vary *quantitatively* ; it may also seem probable that it has more than one *quality* (in the nature of amplitude, for instance). As a new factor we have taken into consideration Breuer's hypothesis that charges of energy occur in two forms [see page 31]; so that we have to distinguish between two kinds of cathexis of the psychical systems or their elements—a freely flowing cathexis that presses on towards discharge and a quiescent cathexis. We may perhaps suspect that the 'binding' of the energy that streams into the mental apparatus consists in its conversion from a freely flowing into a quiescent state.

We may, I think, tentatively venture to regard the common traumatic neurosis as a consequence of an extensive breach being made in the protective shield against stimuli. This would seem to reinstate the old, naive theory of shock, in apparent contrast to the later and psychologically more pretentious theory which attributes aetiological importance not to the effects of mechanical violence but to fright and the threat to life. These opposing views are not, however, irreconcilable; nor is the psycho-analytic view of the traumatic neurosis identical with the shock theory in its crudest form. The latter regards the essence of the shock as being the direct damage to the molecular structure or even to the histological structure of the elements of the nervous system; whereas what *we* seek to understand are the effects produced on the organ of the mind by the breach in the shield against stimuli and by the problems that follow in its train. But we too attribute import-ance to the element of fright. It is caused by the absence of any preparedness for anxiety, including a hypercathexis of the systems that would be the first to receive the stimulus. Owing to their low cathexis those systems are not in a good position for binding the inflowing amounts of excitation and the consequences of the breach in the protective shield follow all the more easily. It will be seen, then, that preparedness for anxiety and the hypercathexis of the receptive systems constitute the last line of defence of the shield against stimuli. In the case of quite a number of traumas, the difference between systems that are unprepared and systems that are well prepared through being hypercathected may be a decisive factor in determining the outcome ; though where the strength of a trauma exceeds a certain limit this factor will no doubt cease to carry weight. The fulfilment of wishes is, as we know, brought about in a hallucinatory manner by dreams, and under the dominance of the pleasure principle this has become their function. But it is not in the service of that principle that the dreams of patients suffering from traumatic neuroses lead them . back with such regularity to the situation in which the trauma occurred. We may assume, rather, that dreams are here helping to carry out another task, which must be accomplished before the dominance of the pleasure principle can even begin. These dreams are endeavouring to master the stimulus retrospectively, by developing the anxiety whose omission was the cause of the traumatic neurosis.[22] They thus afford us a view of a function of the mental apparatus which, though it does not contradict the

[22][Freud is here implicitly stating that the development of anxiety is the means of producing preparedness for anxiety.]

pleasure principle, is nevertheless independent of it and seems to be more primitive than the purpose of gaining pleasure and avoiding unpleasure.

This would seem to be the place, then, at which to admit for the first time an exception to the proposition that dreams are fulfilments of wishes. Anxiety dreams, as I have shown repeatedly and in detail, offer no such exception. Nor do 'punishment dreams,' for they merely replace the forbidden wish-fulfilment by the appropriate punishment for it ; that is to say, they fulfil the wish of the sense of guilt which is the reaction to the repudiated impulse. But it is impossible to classify as wish-fulfilments the dreams we have been discussing which occur in traumatic neuroses, or the dreams during psycho-analyses which bring to memory the psychical traumas of childhood. They arise, rather, in obedience to the compulsion to repeat, though it is true that in analysis that compulsion is supported by the wish (which is encouraged by 'suggestion')[23] to conjure up what has been forgotten and repressed. Thus it would seem that the function of dreams, which consists in setting aside any motives that might interrupt sleep, by fulfilling the wishes of the disturbing impulses, is not their *original* function. It would not be possible for them to perform that function until the whole of mental life had accepted the dominance of the pleasure principle. If there is a 'beyond the pleasure principle,' it is only con-

---

[23][The clause in brackets was substituted in 1923 for the words 'which is not unconscious' which appeared in the earlier editions.]

sistent to grant that there was also a time before the purpose of dreams was the fulfilment of wishes. This would imply no denial of their later function. But if once this general rule has been broken, a further question arises. May not dreams which, with a view to the psychical binding of traumatic impressions, obey the compulsion to repeat—may not such dreams occur *outside* analysis as well ? And the reply can only be a decided affirmative.

I have argued elsewhere[24] that the 'war neuroses' (in so far as that term implies something more than a reference to the circumstances of the illness's onset) may very well be traumatic neuroses which have been facilitated by a conflict in the ego. The fact to which I have referred on page 10, that a gross physical injury caused simultaneously by the trauma diminishes the chances that a neurosis will develop, becomes intelligible if one bears in mind two facts which have been stressed by psycho-analytic research : firstly, that mechanical agitation must be recognized as one of the sources of sexual excitation[25], and secondly, that painful and feverish illnesses exercise a powerful effect, so long as they last, on the distribution of libido. Thus, on the one hand, the mechanical violence of the trauma would liberate a quantity of sexual excitation which, owing to the lack of preparation for anxiety, would have a traumatic effect ; but, on the other hand, the simul-

---

[24]See Freud, 1919 [English translation, 1950, 85].

[25]Cf. my remarks elsewhere (1905 [English translation, 1949, 79 f.]) on the effect of swinging and railway-travel.

taneous physical injury, by calling for a narcissistic hypercathexis of the injured organ,[26] would bind the excess of excitation. It is also well known, though the libido theory has not yet made sufficient use of the fact, that such severe disorders in the distribution of libido as melancholia are temporarily brought to an end by intercurrent organic illness, and indeed that even a fully developed condition of dementia praecox is capable of a temporary remission in these same circumstances.

---

[26]See Freud, 1914a [English translation, 1925, 39 ff].

V

The fact that the cortical layer which receives stimuli is without any protective shield against excitations from within must have as its result that these latter transmissions of stimulus have a preponderance in economic importance and often occasion economic disturbances comparable with traumatic neuroses. The most abundant sources of this internal excitation are what are described as the organism's 'instincts'—the representatives of all the forces originating in the interior of the body and transmitted to the mental apparatus—at once the most important and the most obscure element of psychological research.

It will perhaps not be thought too rash to suppose that the impulses arising from the instincts do not belong to the type of *bound* nervous processes but to the type of *mobile* processes which press towards discharge. The best part of what we know of these processes is derived from our study of the dream-activity. We there discovered that the processes in the unconscious systems were fundamentally different from those in the preconscious (or conscious) systems. In the unconscious, cathexes can easily be completely transferred, displaced and condensed. Such treatment, however, could only produce invalid results if it were applied to preconscious material ;

and this accounts for the familiar peculiarities exhibited by manifest dreams after the preconscious residues of the preceding day have been worked over in accordance with the laws operating in the unconscious. I described the type of process found in the unconscious as the ' primary ' psychical process, in contradistinction to the ' secondary ' process which is the one obtaining in our normal waking life. Since all instinctual impulses have the unconscious systems as their point of impact, it is hardly an innovation to say that they obey the primary process. Again, it is not difficult to identify the primary psychical process with Breuer's mobile cathexis and the secondary process with changes in his bound or tonic cathexis.[27] If so, it would be the task of the higher strata of the mental apparatus to bind the instinctual excitation reaching the primary process. A failure to effect this binding would provoke a disturbance analogous to a traumatic neurosis ; and only after the binding has been accomplished would it be possible for the dominance of the pleasure principle (and of its modification, the reality principle) to proceed unhindered. Till then the other task of the mental apparatus, the task of mastering or binding excitations, would have precedence—not, indeed, in *opposition* to the pleasure principle, but independently of it and to some extent in disregard of it.

---

[27]Cf. my *Interpretation of Dreams* (1900), Chapter VII, [Section E ; English translation, 1932, 549 ff. Cf. also Breuer and Freud, 1895, 167 ff.]

The manifestations of a compulsion to repeat (which we have described as occurring in the early activities of infantile mental life as well as among the events of psycho-analytic treatment) exhibit to a high degree an instinctual character and, when they act in opposition to the pleasure principle, give the appearance of some extraneous force at work. In the case of children's play we seemed to see that children repeat unpleasurable experiences for the additional reason that they can master a powerful impression far more thoroughly by being active than they could by merely experiencing it passively. Each fresh repetition seems to strengthen the mastery they are in search of. Nor can children have their *pleasurable* experiences repeated often enough, and they are inexorable in their insistence that the repetition shall be an identical one. This character trait disappears later on. If a joke is heard for a second time it produces almost no effect ; a theatrical production never creates so great an impression the second time as the first ; indeed, it is hardly possible to persuade an adult who has very much enjoyed reading a book to re-read it immediately. Novelty is always the condition of enjoyment. But children will never tire of asking an adult to repeat a game that he has shown them or played with them, till he is too exhausted to go on. And if a child has been told a nice story, he will insist on hearing it over and over again rather than a new one ; and he will remorselessly stipulate that the repetition shall be an identical one and will correct any alterations of which the narrator may be guilty—though they may actually have been made in the hope of gaining fresh approval. None of this contradicts the pleasure principle ; repetition, the re-experiencing of something identical, is clearly in itself a source of pleasure. In the case of a person in analysis, on the contrary, the compulsion to repeat the events of his childhood in the transference evidently disregards the pleasure principle in every way. The patient behaves in a purely infantile fashion and thus shows us that the repressed memory-traces of his primaeval experiences are not present in him in a bound state and are indeed in a sense incapable of obeying the secondary process. It is to this fact of not being bound, moreover, that they owe their capacity for forming, in conjunction with the residues of the previous day, a wishful phantasy that emerges in a dream. This same compulsion to repeat frequently meets us as an obstacle to our treatment when at the end of an analysis we try to induce the patient to detach himself completely from his physician. It may be presumed, too, that when people unfamiliar with analysis feel an obscure fear—a dread of rousing something that, so they feel, is better left sleeping—what they are afraid of at bottom is the emergence of this compulsion with its hint of possession by some extraneous power.

But how is the predicate of being ' instinctual ' related to the compulsion to repeat ? At this point we cannot escape a suspicion that we may have come upon the track of a universal attribute of the instincts and perhaps of organic life in general which has not hitherto been clearly recognized or at least not explicitly stressed.[28] It seems, then, that an instinct is a compulsion inherent in organic life to restore an earlier state of things[29] which the living entity has been obliged to abandon under the pressure of external disturbing forces; that is, it is a kind of organic elasticity, or, to put it another way, the expression of the inertia inherent in organic life.[30]

This view of instincts strikes us as strange because we have become used to see in them a factor impelling towards change and development, whereas we are now asked to recognize in them the precise contrary—an expression of the *conservative* nature of living substance. On the other hand we soon call to mind examples from animal life which seem to confirm the view that instincts are historically determined. Certain fishes, for instance, undertake laborious migrations at spawning-time in order to deposit their spawn in particular waters far removed from their customary haunts. In the opinion of many biologists what they are doing is merely to seek out the localities in which their species formerly resided but which in the course of time they have exchanged for others. The same explanation is believed to apply to the migratory flights of birds of passage—but we are quickly relieved of the necessity for

---

[28][The last six words were added in 1921.]

[29][This first portion of the sentence is in spaced type in the original.]

[30]I have no doubt that similar notions as to the nature of 'instincts' have already been put forward repeatedly.

seeking for further examples by the reflection that the most impressive proofs of there being an organic compulsion to repeat lie in the phenomena of heredity and the facts of embryology. We see how the germ of a living animal is obliged in the course of its development to recapitulate (even if only in a transient and abbreviated fashion) the structures of all the forms from which it is sprung, instead of proceeding quickly by the shortest path to its final shape. This behaviour is only to a very slight degree attributable to mechanical causes, and the historical explanation cannot accordingly be neglected. So too the power of regenerating a lost organ by growing afresh a precisely similar one, extends far up into the animal kingdom.

We shall be met by the plausible objection that it may very well be that, in addition to the conservative instincts which impel towards repetition, there may be others which push forward towards progress and the production of new forms. This argument must certainly not be overlooked, and it will be taken into account at a later stage.[31] But for the moment it is tempting to pursue the hypothesis that all instincts tend towards the restoration of an earlier state of things to its logical conclusion. The outcome may give an impression of mysticism or of sham profundity ; but we can feel quite innocent of having had any such purpose in view. We seek only for the sober results of research or of reflection based on it ; and

---

[31] [The last half of this sentence was added in 1921.]

we have no wish to find in those results any quality other than certainty.[32]

Let us suppose, then, that all the organic instincts are conservative, are acquired historically and tend towards the restoration of an earlier state of things. It follows that the phenomena of organic development must be attributed to external disturbing and diverting influences. The elementary living entity would from its very beginning have had no wish to change ; if conditions remained the same, it would do no more than constantly repeat the same course of life. In the last resort, what has left its mark on the development of organisms must be the history of the earth we live in and of its relation to the sun. Every modification which is thus imposed upon the course of the organism's life is accepted by the conservative organic instincts and stored up for further repetition. Those instincts are therefore bound to give a deceptive appearance of being forces tending towards change and progress, whilst in fact they are merely seeking to reach an ancient goal by paths alike old and new. Moreover it is possible to specify this final goal of all organic striving. It would be in contradiction to the conservative nature of the instincts if the goal of life were a state of things which had never yet been attained. On the contrary, it must be an *old* state of things, an initial state from which the living

---

[32][Footnote added 1925 :] The reader should not overlook the fact that what follows is the development of an extreme line of thought. Later on, when account is taken of the sexual instincts, it will be found that the necessary limitations and corrections are applied to it.

entity has at one time or other departed and to which it is striving to return by the circuitous paths along which its development leads. If we are to take it as a truth that knows no exception that everything living dies for *internal* reasons—becomes inorganic once again—then we shall be compelled to say that ' the goal of all life is death ' and, looking backwards, that ' what was inanimate existed before what is living.'[33]

The attributes of life were at some time evoked in inanimate matter by the action of a force of whose nature we can form no conception. It may perhaps have been a process similar in type to that which later caused the development of consciousness in a particular stratum of living matter. The tension which then arose in what had hitherto been an inanimate substance endeavoured to equalize its potential. In this way the first instinct came into being : the instinct to return to the inanimate state. It was still an easy matter at that time for a living substance to die ; the course of its life was probably only a brief one, whose direction was determined by the chemical structure of the young life. For a long time, perhaps, living substance was thus being constantly created afresh and easily dying, till decisive external influences altered in such a way as to oblige the still surviving substance to diverge ever more widely from its original course of life and to make ever more complicated détours before reaching its goal in death. These circuitous paths to

---

[33][The phrases in inverted commas are in spaced type in the original.]

death, faithfully kept to by the conservative instincts, would present us to-day with the picture of the phenomena of life. If we firmly maintain the exclusively conservative nature of instincts, we cannot arrive at any other notions as to the origin and goal of life.

The implications in regard to the great groups of instincts which, as we believe, lie behind the phenomena of life in organisms must appear no less bewildering. The hypothesis of self-preservative instincts, such as we attribute to all living beings, stands in marked opposition to the idea that instinctual life as a whole serves to bring about death. Seen in this light, the theoretical importance of the instincts of self-preservation, of self-assertion and of mastery greatly diminishes. They are component instincts whose function it is to assure that the organism shall follow its own path to death, and to ward off any possible ways of returning to inorganic existence other than those which are immanent in the organism itself. We have no longer to reckon with the organism's puzzling determination (so hard to fit into any context) to maintain its own existence in the face of every obstacle. What we are left with is the fact that the organism wishes to die only in its own fashion. Thus these guardians of life, too, were originally the myrmidons of death. Hence arises the paradoxical situation that the living organism struggles most energetically against events (dangers, in fact) which might help it to attain its life's goal rapidly—by a kind of short-circuit. Such behaviour is however precisely what characterizes instinctual as contrasted with intelligent efforts.[34]

But let us pause for a moment and reflect. It cannot be so. The sexual instincts, to which the theory of the neuroses gives a quite special place, appear under a very different aspect.

The external pressure which provokes a constantly increasing extent of development has not imposed itself upon *every* organism. Many have succeeded in remaining up to the present time at their lowly level. Many, if not all, of such creatures, which are living to-day, must resemble the earliest stages of the higher animals and plants. In the same way, the whole path of development to natural death is not trodden by *all* the elementary entities which compose the complicated body of one of the higher organisms. Some of them, the germ-cells, probably retain the original structure of living matter and, after a certain time, with their full complement of inherited and freshly acquired instinctual dispositions, separate themselves from the organism as a whole. These two characteristics may be precisely what enables them to have an independent existence. Under favourable conditions, they begin to develop—that is, to repeat the performance to which they owe their existence ; and in the end once again one portion of their substance pursues its development to a finish, while another portion harks back once

---

[34][In the editions before 1925 the following footnote appeared at this point. ' A correction of this extreme view of the self-preservative instincts follows '].

again as a fresh residual germ to the beginning of the process of development. These germ-cells, therefore, work against the death of the living substance and succeed in winning for it what we can only regard as potential immortality, though that may mean no more than a lengthening of the road to death. We must regard as in the highest degree significant the fact that this function of the germ-cell is reinforced, or only made possible, if it coalesces with another cell similar to itself and yet differing from it.

The instincts which watch over the destinies of these elementary organisms that survive the whole individual, which provide them with a safe shelter while they are defenceless against the stimuli of the external world, which bring about their meeting with other germ-cells, and so on—these constitute the group of the sexual instincts. They are conservative in the same sense as the other instincts in that they bring back earlier states of living substance ; but they are conservative to a higher degree in that they are peculiarly resistent to external influences ; and they are conservative too in another sense in that they preserve life itself for a comparatively long period.[35] They are the true life instincts. They operate against the purpose of the other instincts, which leads, by reason of their function, to death ; and this fact indicates that there is an opposition between them

---

[35][Footnote added 1923 :] Yet it is to them alone that we can attribute an internal impulse towards ' progress ' and towards higher development ! (See below [page 56].)

and the other instincts, an opposition whose importance was long ago recognized by the theory of the
neuroses. It is as though the life of the organism
moved with a vacillating rhythm. One group of
instincts rushes forward so as to reach the final goal
of life as swiftly as possible ; but when a particular
stage in the advance has been reached, the other
group jerks back to a certain point to make a fresh
start and so prolong the journey. And even though
it is certain that sexuality and the distinction between
the sexes did not exist when life began, the possibility
remains that the instincts which were later to be
described as sexual may have been in operation
from the very first, and it may not be true that it
was only at a later time that they started upon their
work of opposing the activities of the ' ego instincts.'[36]

Let us now hark back for a moment ourselves
and consider whether there is any basis at all for these
speculations. Is it really the case that, apart from the
sexual instincts,[37] there are no instincts that do not
seek to restore an earlier state of things ? that there
are none that aim at a state of things which has never
yet been attained ? I know of no certain example
from the organic world that would contradict the
characterization I have thus proposed. There is
unquestionably no universal instinct towards higher

---

[36][Footnote added 1925 :] It should be understood from the
context that the term ' ego instincts ' is used here as a provisional
description and derives from the earliest psycho-analytical
terminology.

[37][These five words were printed in spaced type from 1921
onwards.]

development observable in the animal or plant world, even though it is undeniable that development does in fact occur in that direction. But on the one hand it is often merely a matter of opinion when we declare that one stage of development is higher than another, and on the other hand biology teaches us that higher development in one respect is very frequently balanced or outweighed by involution in another. Moreover there are plenty of animal forms from whose early stages we can infer that their development has, on the contrary, assumed a retrograde character. Both higher development and involution might well be the consequences of adaptation to the pressure of external forces ; and in both cases the part played by instincts might be limited to the retention (in the form of an internal source of pleasure) of an obligatory modification.[38]

It may be difficult, too, for many of us, to abandon the belief that there is an instinct towards perfection at work in human beings, which has brought them to their present high level of intellectual achievement and ethical sublimation and which may be expected to watch over their development into supermen. I have no faith, however, in the existence of any such internal instinct and I cannot see how this benevolent

---

[38]Ferenczi (1913, 137) has reached the same conclusion along different lines : ' If this thought is pursued to its logical conclusion, one must make oneself familiar with the idea of a tendency to perseveration or regression dominating organic life as well, while the tendency to further development, to adaptation, etc., would become active only as a result of external stimuli.' [English translation, 1916 (modified), 237 n.]

illusion is to be preserved. The present development of human beings requires, as it seems to me, no different explanation from that of animals. What appears in a minority of human individuals as an untiring impulsion towards further perfection can easily be understood as a result of the instinctual repression upon which is based all that is most precious in human civilization. The repressed instinct never ceases to strive for complete satisfaction, which would consist in the repetition of a primary experience of satisfaction. No substitutive or reactive formations and no sublimations will suffice to remove the repressed instinct's persisting tension ; and it is the difference in amount between the gratificatory pleasure which is demanded and that which is actually achieved that provides the driving factor which will permit of no halting at any established position but, in the poet's words, ' *ungebändigt immer vorwärts dringt.*'[39] The backward path that leads to complete satisfaction is as a rule obstructed by the resistances which maintain the repressions. So there is no alternative but to advance in the direction in which growth is still free—though with no prospect of bringing the process to a conclusion or of being able to reach the goal. The processes involved in the formation of a neurotic phobia, which is nothing else than an attempt at flight from the satisfaction of an instinct, present us with a model of the manner of origin of this supposititious ' instinct towards

[39][' Presses ever forward unsubdued.'] Mephistopheles in *Faust*, Part I.

perfection'—an instinct which cannot possibly be attributed to *every* human being. The *dynamic* conditions for its development are, indeed, universally present ; but it is only in rare cases that the *economic* situation appears to favour the production of the phenomenon.

I will add only a word to suggest that the efforts of Eros to combine organic substances into ever larger unities probably provide a substitute for this ' instinct towards perfection ' whose existence we cannot admit. The phenomena that are attributed to it seem capable of explanation by these efforts of Eros taken in conjunction with the results of repression.[40]

---

[40][This paragraph was added in 1923.]

VI

The upshot of our enquiry so far has been the drawing of a sharp distinction between the ' ego instincts ' and the sexual instincts, and the view that the former exercise a thrust towards death and the latter towards a prolongation of life. But this conclusion is bound to be unsatisfactory in many respects even to ourselves. Moreover, it is actually only of the former group of instincts that we can predicate a conservative, or rather retrograde, character corresponding to a compulsion to repeat. For on our hypothesis the ego instincts arise from the coming to life of inanimate matter and they seek to restore the inanimate state ; whereas as regards the sexual instincts, though it is true that they re- produce primitive states of the organism, what they are clearly aiming at by every possible means is the coalescence of two germ-cells which are differen- tiated in a particular way. If this union is not effected, the germ-cell dies along with all the other elements of the multicellular organism. It is only on this condition that the sexual function can prolong the cell's life and lend it the appearance of immortality. But what is the important event in the development of living substance which is being repeated in sexual reproduction, or in its fore-runner, the conjugation of two protista ? We cannot say ; and we should consequently feel relieved if the whole structure of our argument turned out to be mistaken. The opposition between the ego or death instincts and the sexual or life instincts would then cease to hold and the compulsion to repeat would no longer possess the importance we have ascribed to it.

Let us turn back, then, to one of the assumptions that we have already made, with the expectation that we shall be able to give it a categorical denial. We have drawn far-reaching conclusions from the hypothesis that all living substance is bound to die from internal causes. We made this assumption thus carelessly because it does not seem to us to *be* an assumption. We are accustomed to think that such is the fact, and we are strengthened in our thought by the writings of our poets. Perhaps we have adopted the belief because there is some comfort in it. If we are to die ourselves, and first to lose in death those who are dearest to us, it is easier to submit to a remorseless law of nature, to the sublime Ἀνάγκη [Necessity], than to a chance which might perhaps have been escaped. It may be, however, that this belief in the internal necessity of dying is only another of those illusions which we have created ' um die Schwere des Daseins zu ertragen.'[41] It is certainly not a primaeval belief. The notion of ' natural death ' is quite foreign to primitive races ; they attribute every death that occurs among them to the influence of an enemy or of an evil spirit.

---

[41]['To bear the burden of existence. (Schiller, *Braut von Messina*, Act I).]

5

We must therefore turn to biology in order to test the validity of the belief.

If we do so, we may be astonished to find how little agreement there is among biologists on the subject of natural death and in fact that the whole concept of death melts away under their hands. The fact that there is a fixed average duration of life at least among the higher animals naturally argues in favour of there being such a thing as death from natural causes. But this impression is countered when we consider that certain large animals and certain gigantic arboreal growths reach a very advanced age and one which cannot at present be computed. According to the grandiose conception of Wilhelm Fliess [1906], all the vital phenomena exhibited by organisms—including, no doubt, their death—are linked with the completion of fixed periods, which express the dependence of two kinds of living substance (one male and the other female) upon the solar year. When we see, however, how easily and how extensively the influence of external forces is able to modify the date of the appearance of vital phenomena (especially in the plant world)— to precipitate them or hold them back—doubts must be cast upon the rigidity of Fliess's formulas or at least upon whether the laws laid down by him are the sole determining factors.

The greatest interest attaches from our point of view to the treatment given to the subject of the duration of life and the death of organisms in the writings of Weismann (1882, 1884, 1892, etc.) It was he who introduced the division of living substance into mortal and immortal parts. The mortal part is the body in the narrower sense—the 'soma'—which alone is subject to natural death. The germ-cells, on the other hand, are potentially immortal, in so far as they are able, under certain favourable conditions, to develop into a new individual, or, in other words, to surround themselves with a new soma. (Weismann, 1884.)

What strikes us in this is the unexpected analogy with our own view, which was arrived at along such a different path. Weismann, regarding living substance morphologically, sees in it one portion which is destined to die—the soma, the body apart from the substance concerned with sex and inheritance—and an immortal portion—the germ-plasm, which is concerned with the survival of the species, with reproduction. We, on the other hand, dealing not with the living substance but with the forces operating in it, have been led to distinguish two kinds of instincts : those which seek to lead what is living to death, and others, the sexual instincts, which are perpetually attempting and achieving a renewal of life. This sounds like a dynamic corollary to Weismann's morphological theory.

But the appearance of a significant correspondence is dissipated as soon as we discover Weismann's views on the problem of death. For he only relates the distinction between the mortal soma and the immortal germ-plasm to *multicellular* organisms ; in unicellular organisms the individual and the reproductive cell are still one and the same (Weismann, 1882, 38). Thus he considers that unicellular organisms are potentially immortal, and that death only makes its appearance with the multicellular metazoa. It is true that this death of the higher organisms is a natural one, a death from internal causes ; but it is not founded upon any primal characteristic of living substance (Weismann, 1884, 84) and cannot be regarded as an absolute necessity with its basis in the very nature of life (Weismann, 1882, 33). Death is rather a matter of expediency, a manifestation of adaptation to the external conditions of life ; for, when once the cells of the body have been divided into soma and germ-plasm, an unlimited duration of individual life would become a quite pointless luxury. When this differentiation had been made in the multicellular organisms, death became possible and expedient. Since then the soma of the higher organisms has died at fixed periods for internal reasons, while the protista have remained immortal. It is not the case, on the other hand, that reproduction was only introduced at the same time as death. On the contrary, it is a primal characteristic of living matter, like growth (from which it originated), and life has been continuous from its first beginning upon earth. (Weismann, 1884, 84f.)

It will be seen at once that to concede in this way that higher organisms have a natural death is of very little help to us. If death is a late acquisition of organisms, then there can be no question of there having been death instincts from the very beginning of life on this earth. Multicellular organisms may die for internal reasons, owing to defective differentiation or to imperfections in their metabolism, but the matter is of no interest from the point of view of our problem. An account of the origin of death such as this is moreover far less at variance with our habitual modes of thought than the strange assumption of ' death instincts.'

The discussion which followed upon Weismann's suggestions led, so far as I can see, to no conclusive results in any direction.[42] Some writers returned to the views of Goette (1883), who regarded death as a direct result of reproduction. Hartmann (1906, 29) does not regard the appearance of a ' dead body '— a dead portion of the living substance—as the criterion of death, but defines death as ' the termination of individual development.' In this sense protozoa too are mortal ; in their case death always coincides with reproduction, but is to some extent obscured by it, since the whole substance of the parent animal may be transmitted directly into the young offspring.

Soon afterwards research was directed to the experimental testing upon unicellular organisms of the alleged immortality of living substance. An American biologist, Woodruff, experimenting with a ciliate infusorian, the ' slipper-animalcule,' which reproduces by fission into two individuals, persisted until the 3029th generation (at which point he broke off the experiment), isolating one of the part products on each occasion and placing it in fresh water.

---

[42]Cf. Hartmann (1906), Lipschütz (1914) and Doflein (1919).

This remote descendent of the first slipper-animalcule was just as lively as its ancestor and showed no signs of ageing or degeneration. Thus, in so far as figures of this kind prove anything, the immortality of the protista seemed to be experimentally demonstrable.[43]

Other experimenters arrived at different results. Maupas, Calkins and others, in contrast to Woodruff, found that after a certain number of divisions these infusoria become weaker, diminish in size, suffer the loss of some part of their organization and eventually die, unless certain recuperative measures are applied to them. If this is so, protozoa would appear to die after a phase of senescence exactly like the higher animals—thus completely contradicting Weismann's assertion that death is a late acquisition of living organisms.

From the aggregate of these experiments two facts emerge which seem to offer us a firm footing.

First : If two of the animalculae, at the moment before they show signs of senescence, are able to coalesce with each other, that is to ' conjugate,' (soon after which they once more separate), they are saved from growing old and become ' rejuvenated.' Conjugation is no doubt the fore-runner of the sexual reproduction of higher creatures ; it is as yet unconnected with propagation and is limited to the mixing of the substances of the two individuals. (Weismann's ' amphimixis.') The recuperative effects of conjugation can, however, be replaced by certain stimulating agents, by alterations in the composition

---

[43]For this and what follows see Lipschütz (1914, 26 and 52 ff.).

of the fluid which provides their nourishment, by raising their temperature or by shaking them. We are reminded of the celebrated experiment made by J. Loeb, in which, by means of certain chemical stimuli he induced segmentation in sea-urchins' eggs—a process which can normally occur only after fertilization.

Secondly : It is probable nevertheless that infusoria die a natural death as a result of their own vital processes. For the contradiction between Woodruff's findings and the others is due to his having provided each generation with fresh nutrient fluid. If he omitted to do so, he observed the same signs of senescence as the other experimenters. He concluded that the animalculae were injured by the products of metabolism which they extruded into the surrounding fluid. He was then able to prove conclusively that it was only the products of its *own* metabolism which had fatal results for a particular generation. For the same animalculae which inevitably perished if they were crowded together in their own nutrient fluid flourished in a solution which was over-saturated with the waste products of a distantly related species. An infusorian, therefore, if it is left to itself, dies a natural death owing to its incomplete voidance of the products of its own metabolism. It may be, however, that the same incapacity is the ultimate cause of the death of all higher animals as well.

At this point the question may well arise in our minds whether any object whatever is served by trying to solve the problem of natural death from a study of the protozoa. The primitive organization of these creatures may conceal from our eyes important conditions which, though in fact present in them too, only become *visible* in higher animals where they are able to find morphological expression. And if we abandon the morphological point of view and adopt the dynamic one, it becomes a matter of complete indifference to us whether natural death can be shown to occur in protozoa or not. The substance which is later recognized as being immortal has not yet become separated in them from the mortal one. The instinctual forces which seek to conduct life into death may also be operating in protozoa from the first, and yet their effects may be so completely concealed by the life-preserving forces that it may be very hard to find any direct evidence of their presence. We have seen, moreover, that the observations made by biologists allow us to assume that internal processes of this kind leading to death do occur also in protista. But even if protista turned out to be immortal in Weismann's sense, his assertion that death is a late acquisition would apply only to its *manifest* phenomena and would not make impossible the assumption of processes *tending* towards it.

Thus our expectation that biology would flatly contradict the recognition of death instincts has not been fulfilled. We are at liberty to continue concerning ourselves with their possibility, if we have other reasons for doing so. The striking similarity between Weismann's distinction of soma and germ-plasm and our separation of the death instincts from the life instincts persists and retains its significance. Let us pause for a moment over this pre-eminently dualistic view of instinctual life. According to E. Hering's theory, two kinds of processes are constantly at work in living substance, operating in contrary directions, one constructive or assimilatory and the other destructive or dissimilatory. May we venture to recognize in these two directions taken by the vital processes the activity of our two instinctual impulses, the life instincts and the death instincts? There is something else, at any rate, that we cannot remain blind to. We have unwittingly steered our course into the harbour of Schopenhauer's philosophy. For him death is the ' true result and to that extent the purpose of life,'[44] while the sexual instinct is the embodiment of the will to live.

Let us make a bold attempt at another step forward. It is generally considered that the union of a number of cells into a vital association—the multicellular character of organisms—has become a means of prolonging their life. One cell helps to preserve the life of another, and the community of cells can survive even if individual cells have to die. We have already heard that conjugation, too, the temporary coalescence of two unicellular organisms, has a life-preserving and rejuvenating effect on both of them. Accordingly, we might attempt to apply the libido theory which has been arrived at in psycho-

---

[44]Schopenhauer (1851 ; *Sämtliche Werke*, ed. Hübscher 1938, **5**, 236).

analysis to the mutual relationship of cells. We might suppose that the life instincts or sexual instincts which are active in each cell take the other cells as their object, that they partly neutralize the death instincts (*i.e.* the processes set up by them) in those other cells and thus preserve their life ; while the other cells do the same for *them*, and still others sacrifice themselves in the performance of this libidinal function. The germ-cells themselves would behave in a completely 'narcissistic' fashion— to use the phrase that we are accustomed to use in the theory of the neuroses to describe a whole indivi- dual who retains his libido in his ego and pays none of it out in object-cathexes. The germ-cells require their libido, the activity of their life instincts, for themselves, as a reserve against their later momentous constructive activity. (The cells of the malignant neoplasms which destroy the organism should also perhaps be described as narcissistic in this same sense : pathology is prepared to regard their germs as innate and to ascribe embryonic attributes to them.[45]) In this way the libido of our sexual instincts would coincide with the Eros of the poets and philosophers which binds all living things together.

Here then is an opportunity for looking back over the slow development of our libido theory. In the first instance the analysis of the transference neuroses forced upon our notice the opposition between the 'sexual instincts,' which are directed towards an object, and certain other instincts, with

---

[45][This sentence was added in 1921.]

which we were very insufficiently acquainted and which we described provisionally as the ' ego instincts.' A foremost place among these was necessarily given to the instincts serving the self-preservation of the individual. It was impossible to say what other distinctions were to be drawn among them. No knowledge would have been more valuable as a foundation for true psychological knowledge than an approximate grasp of the common characteristics and possible distinctive features of the instincts. But in no region of psychology were we groping more in the dark. Everyone assumed the existence of as many instincts or ' basic instincts ' as he chose, and juggled with them like the ancient Greek natural philosophers with their four elements—earth, air, fire and water. Psycho-analysis, which could not escape making *some* assumption about the instincts, kept at first to the popular division of instincts typified in the phrase ' hunger and love.' At least there was nothing arbitrary in this ; and by its help the analysis of the psycho-neuroses was carried forward quite a distance. The concept of ' sexuality,' and at the same time of the sexual instinct, had, it is true, to be extended so as to cover many things which could not be classed under the reproductive function ; and this caused no little hubbub in an austere, respectable or merely hypocritical world.

The next step was taken when psycho-analysis felt its way closer towards the ego of psychology, which it had first come to know only as a repressive, censoring agency, capable of erecting protective structures and reactive formations. Critical and far-seeing minds had, it is true, long since objected to the concept of libido being restricted to the energy of the sexual instincts directed towards an object. But they failed to explain how they had arrived at their better knowledge or to derive from it anything of which analysis could make use. Advancing more cautiously, psycho-analysis observed the regularity with which libido is withdrawn from the object and directed on to the ego (the process of introversion) ; and, by studying the libidinal development of children in its earliest phases, came to the conclusion that the ego is the true and original reservoir of libido, and that it is only from that reservoir that libido is extended on to objects. The ego found its way among the child's sexual objects and was at once given the foremost place among them. Libido which was in this way lodged in the ego was described as ' narcissistic.' (Cf. Freud, 1914*a*). This narcissistic libido was of course also a manifestation of the force of the sexual instinct in the analytical sense of those words, and it had necessarily to be identified with the ' self-preservative instincts ' whose existence had been recognized from the first. Thus the original opposition between the ego instincts and the sexual instincts proved to be inadequate. A portion of the ego instincts was seen to be libidinal ; sexual instincts —probably alongside others—operated in the ego. Nevertheless we are justified in saying that the old formula which lays it down that psycho-neuroses are based on a conflict between ego instincts and sexual instincts contains nothing that we need reject to-day. It is merely that the distinction between the two kinds of instinct, which was originally regarded as in some sort of way *qualitative*, must now be characterized differently— namely as being *topographical*. And in particular it is still true that the transference neuroses, the essential subject of psycho-analytic study, are the result of a conflict between the ego and the libidinal cathexis of objects.

But it is all the more necessary for us to lay stress upon the libidinal character of the self-preservative instincts now that we are venturing upon the further step of recognizing the sexual instinct as Eros, the preserver of all things, and of deriving the narcissistic libido of the ego from the stores of libido by means of which the cells of the soma are attached to one another. But we now find ourselves suddenly faced by another question. If the self-preservative instincts too are of a libidinal nature, are there perhaps no other instincts whatever but the libidinal ones? At all events there are none other visible. But in that case we shall after all be driven to agree with the critics who suspected from the first that psycho-analysis explains *everything* by sexuality, or with innovators like Jung who, making a hasty judgement, have used the word ' libido ' to mean instinctual force in general. Must not this be so?

It was not our *intention* at all events to produce such a result. Our argument had as its point of departure a sharp distinction between ego instincts,

which we equated with death instincts, and sexual
instincts, which we equated with life instincts.
(We were prepared at one stage [page 51] to include
the so-called self-preservative instincts of the ego
among the death instincts ; but we subsequently
[page 53] corrected ourselves on this point and
withdrew it.) Our views have from the very first
been *dualistic*, and to-day they are even more definitely
dualistic than before—now that we describe the
opposition as being, not between ego instincts and
sexual instincts but between life instincts and death
instincts. Jung's libido theory is on the contrary
monistic ; the fact that he has called his one instinctual
force ' libido ' is bound to cause confusion, but need
not affect us otherwise.[46] We suspect that instincts
other than those of self-preservation operate in the
ego, and it ought to be possible for us to point to
them. Unfortunately, however, the analysis of the
ego has made so little headway that it is very difficult
for us to do so. It is possible, indeed, that the libidinal
instincts in the ego may be linked in a peculiar
manner[47] with the other ego instincts which are
still strange to us. Even before we had any clear
understanding of narcissism, psycho-analysts had a
suspicion that the ' ego instincts ' had libidinal
components attached to them. But these are very
uncertain possibilities, to which our opponents will
pay very little attention. The difficulty remains that

---

[46][The two preceding sentences were added in 1921.]

[47][In the first edition only : ' —by instinctual " confluence,"
to borrow a term used by Adler [1908] —'.]

psycho-analysis has not enabled us hitherto to point to any instincts other than the libidinal ones. That, however, is no reason for our falling in with the conclusion that no others in fact exist.

In the obscurity that reigns at present in the theory of the instincts, it would be unwise to reject any idea that promises to throw light on it. We started out from the great opposition between the life and death instincts. Now object-love itself presents us with a second example of a similar polarity—that between love (or affection) and hate (or aggressiveness). If only we could succeed in relating these two polarities to each other and in deriving one from the other! From the very first we recognized the presence of a sadistic component in the sexual instinct.[48] As we know, it can make itself independent and can, in the form of a perversion, dominate an individual's entire sexual activity. It also emerges as a predominant component instinct in one of the ' pregenital organizations', as I have named them. But how can the sadistic instinct, whose aim it is to injure the object, be derived from Eros, the preserver of life? Is it not plausible to suppose that this sadism is in fact a death instinct which, under the influence of the narcissistic libido, has been forced out of the ego and has consequently emerged in relation to the object? It now enters the service of the sexual function. During the oral stage of organization of the libido, the act of obtaining erotic possession

---

[48]This was already so in the first edition of *Three Essays on the Theory of Sexuality* in 1905.

of an object coincides with that object's destruction ; later, the sadistic instinct separates off, and finally, at the stage of genital primacy, it takes on, for the purposes of reproduction, the function of over-powering the sexual object to the extent necessary for carrying out the sexual act. It might indeed be said that the sadism which has been forced out of the ego has pointed the way for the libidinal components of the sexual instinct, and that these follow after it to the object. Wherever the original sadism has undergone no mitigation or intermixture, we find the familiar ambivalence of love and hate in erotic life.

If such an assumption as this is permissible, then we have met the demand that we should produce an example of a death instinct—though it is true that our example is a displaced one. But this way of looking at things is very far from being easy to grasp and creates a positively mystical impression. It looks suspiciously as though we were trying to find a way out of a highly embarrassing situation at any price. We may recall, however, that there is nothing new in an assumption of this kind. We put one forward on an earlier occasion, before there was any question of an embarrassing situation. Clinical observations led us at that time to the view that masochism, the component instinct which is complementary to sadism, must be regarded as sadism that has been turned round upon the subject's own ego.[49] But there is no difference in principle

---

[49]See Freud, 1905 [English translation, 1949, 37] and Freud, 1915a [English translation, 1925, 70 f.].

between an instinct turning from an object to the ego and its turning from the ego to an object—which is the novelty now under discussion. Masochism, the turning round of the instinct upon the object's own ego, would appear in fact to be a return to an earlier phase of the instinct's history, a regression. The account that was then given of masochism would need to be emended for being too sweeping : there *might* be such a thing as primary masochism —a possibility which I had contested at that time.[50]

Let us, however, return to the self-preservative sexual instincts. The experiments upon protista have already shown us that conjugation—that is, the coalescence of two individuals which separate soon afterwards without any subsequent cell-division occurring—has a strengthening and rejuvenating effect upon both of them.[51] In later generations they show no signs of degenerating and seem able to put up a longer resistance to the injurious effects of their own metabolism. This single observation may, I

[50]A considerable portion of these speculations have been anticipated by Sabina Spielrein (1912) in an instructive and interesting paper which, however, is unfortunately not entirely clear to me. She there describes the sadistic components of the sexual instinct as ' destructive.' A. Stärke (1914), again, has attempted to identify the concept of libido itself with the biological concept (assumed on theoretical grounds) of an impetus towards death. See also Rank (1907). All these discussions, like that in the text, give evidence of the demand for a clarification of the theory of the instincts such as has not yet been achieved.

[51] See the account quoted above, page 64, from Lipschütz (1914).

think, be taken as typical of the effect produced by sexual union as well. But how is it that the coalescence of two only slightly different cells can bring about this renewal of life ? The experiment which replaces the conjugation of protozoa by the application of chemical or even of mechanical stimuli (cf. Lipschütz, 1914) enables us to give what is no doubt a conclusive reply to this question. The result is brought about by the influx of fresh amounts of stimulus. This tallies well with the hypothesis that the vital process of the individual leads for internal reasons to an equalization of chemical tensions, that is to say, to death, whereas union with the living substance of a different individual increases those tensions, introducing what may be described as fresh 'vital differences [of potential]' which must then be lived down. As regards these differences there must of course be one or more optima. The dominating tendency of mental life, and perhaps of nervous life in general, is the effort to reduce, to keep constant or to remove internal tension due to stimuli (the 'Nirvana principle,' to borrow a term from Barbara Low [1920, 73])—a tendency which finds expression in the pleasure principle ; and our recognition of that fact is one of our strongest reasons for believing in the existence of death instincts.

But we still feel our line of thought appreciably hampered by the fact that we cannot ascribe to the sexual instinct the characteristic of a compulsion to repeat which first put us on the track of the death instincts. The sphere of embryonic developmental processes is no doubt extremely rich in such phenomena of repetition ; the two germ-cells that are involved in sexual reproduction and their life history are themselves only repetitions of the beginnings of organic life. But the essence of the processes to which sexual life is directed is the coalescence of two cell-bodies. That alone is what guarantees the immortality of the living substance in the higher organisms.

In other words, we need more information on the origin of sexual reproduction and of the sexual instincts in general. This is a problem which is calculated to daunt an outsider and which the specialists themselves have not yet been able to solve. We shall therefore give only the briefest summary of whatever seems relevant to our line of thought from among the many discordant assertions and opinions.

One of these views deprives the problem of reproduction of its mysterious fascination by representing it as a part manifestation of growth. (Cf. multiplication by fission, sprouting or gemmation.) The origin of reproduction by sexually differentiated germ-cells might be pictured along sober Darwinian lines by supposing that the advantage of amphimixis, arrived at on some occasion by the chance conjugation of two protista, was retained and further exploited in later development.[52] On this view ' sex ' would

---

[52]Though Weismann (1892) denies this advantage as well : ' In no case does fertilization correspond to a rejuvenescence or renewal of life, nor is its occurrence necessary in order that life may endure : it is merely an arrangement which renders possible the intermingling of two different hereditary tendencies.' [English translation, 1893, 231.] He nevertheless believes that an intermingling of this kind leads to an increase in the variability of the organism concerned.

not be anything very ancient ; and the extraordinarily violent instincts whose aim it is to bring about sexual union would be repeating something that had once occurred by chance and had since become established as being advantageous.

The question arises here, as in the case of death, whether we are only justified in ascribing to the protista those characteristics which they actually exhibit, and whether it is right to assume that forces and processes which only become visible in the higher organisms first originated in those organisms. The view of sexuality we have just mentioned is of little help for our purposes. The objection may be raised against it that it postulates the existence of life instincts already operating in the simplest organisms ; for otherwise conjugation, which works counter to the course of life and makes the task of ceasing to live more difficult, would not be retained and elaborated but would be avoided. If, therefore, we are not to abandon the hypothesis of death instincts, we must suppose them to be associated from the very first with life instincts. But it must be admitted that in that case we shall be working upon an equation with two unknown quantities.

Apart from this, science has so little to tell us about the origin of sexuality that we can liken the problem to a darkness into which not so much as a ray of an hypothesis has penetrated. In quite a different region, it is true, we *do* meet with such an hypothesis ; but it is of so fantastic a kind—a myth rather than a scientific explanation—that I should not venture to produce it here, were it not that it fulfils precisely the one condition whose fulfilment we desire. For it traces the origin of an instinct to a need to restore an earlier state of things.[53]

What I have in mind is, of course, the theory which Plato put into the mouth of Aristophanes in the *Symposium*, and which deals not only with the *origin* of the sexual instinct but also with the most important of its variations in relation to its object. ' The original human nature was not like the present, but different. In the first place, the sexes were originally three in number, not two as they are now ; there was man, woman, and the union of the two . . . .' Everything about these primaeval men was double : they had four hands and four feet, two faces, two privy parts, and so on. Eventually Zeus decided to cut these men in two, ' like a sorb-apple which is halved for pickling.' After the division had been made, ' the two parts of man, each desiring his other half, came together, and threw their arms about one another eager to grow into one.'[54]

---

[53][The last nine words are in spaced type in the original.]

[54][Jowett's translation. Footnote added 1921 :] I have to thank Professor Heinrich Gomperz, of Vienna, for the following discussion on the origin of the Platonic myth, which I give partly in his own words. It is to be remarked that what is essentially the same theory is already to be found in the Upanishads. For we find the following passage in the *Brihadâranyaka-upanishad*, 1, 4, 3 [Max-Müller's translation, **2**, 85 f.], where the origin of the world from the Atman (the Self or Ego) is described : ' But he felt no delight. Therefore a man who is lonely feels no delight. He wished for a second. He was so large as man and wife together. He then made this his

BEYOND THE PLEASURE PRINCIPLE

Shall we follow the hint given us by the poet-philosopher, and venture upon the hypothesis that living substance at the time of its coming to life was torn apart into small particles, which have ever since endeavoured to reunite through the sexual instincts ? that these instincts, in which the chemical affinity of inanimate matter persisted, gradually succeeded, as they developed through the kingdom of the protista, in overcoming the difficulties put in the way of that endeavour by an environment charged with dangerous stimuli—stimuli which compelled them to form a protective cortical layer ? that these splintered fragments of living substance in this way attained a multicellular condition and finally trans-

Note 54—*continued*.

Self to fall in two, and thence arose husband and wife. Therefore Yagñavalkya said : " We two are thus (each of us) like half a shell." Therefore the void which was there, is filled by the wife.'

The *Brihadâranyaka-upanishad* is the most ancient of all the Upanishads, and no competent authority dates it later than about the year 800 B.C. In contradiction to the prevailing opinion, I should hesitate to give an unqualified denial to the possibility of Plato's myth being derived, even if it were only indirectly, from the Indian source, since a similar possibility cannot be excluded in the case of the doctrine of transmigration. But even if a derivation of this kind (through the Pythagoreans in the first instance) were established, the significance of the coincidence between the two trains of thought would scarcely be diminished. For Plato would not have adopted a story of this kind which had somehow reached him through some oriental tradition—let alone giving it so important a place—unless it had struck him as containing an element of truth.

In a paper devoted to a systematic examination of this line of thought before the time of Plato, Ziegler (1913) traces it back to Babylonian origins.

ferred the instinct for reuniting, in the most highly concentrated form, to the germ-cells ?—But here, I think, the moment has come for breaking off.

Not, however, without the addition of a few words of critical reflection. It may be asked whether and how far I am myself convinced of the truth of the hypotheses that have been set out in these pages. My answer would be that I am not convinced myself and that I do not seek to persuade other people to believe in them. Or, more precisely, that I do not know how far I believe in them. There is no reason, as it seems to me, why the emotional factor of conviction should enter into this question at all. It is surely possible to throw oneself into a line of thought and to follow it wherever it leads out of simple scientific curiosity, or, if the reader prefers, as an *advocatus diaboli*, who is not on that account himself sold to the devil. I do not dispute the fact that the third step in the theory of the instincts, which I have taken here, cannot lay claim to the same degree of certainty as the two earlier ones—the extension of the concept of sexuality and the hypothesis of narcissism. These two innovations were a direct translation of observation into theory and were no more open to sources of error than is inevitable in all such cases. It is true that my assertion of the regressive character of instincts also rests upon observed material—namely on the facts of the compulsion to repeat. It may be, however, that I have overestimated their significance. And in any case it is impossible to pursue an idea of this kind except by repeatedly combining factual material with what is purely speculative and thus diverging widely from observation. The more frequently this is done in the course of constructing a theory, the more untrustworthy, as we know, must be the final result. But the degree of uncertainty is not assignable. One may have made a lucky hit or one may have gone shamefully astray. I do not attach much importance to the part played by what is called 'intuition' in work of this kind. What I have seen of it seems to me rather to be the result of a kind of intellectual impartiality. Unfortunately, however, people are seldom impartial where ultimate things, the great problems of science and life, are concerned. Each of us is governed in such cases by deep-rooted internal prejudices, into whose hands our speculation unwittingly plays. Since we have such good grounds for being distrustful, our attitude towards the results of our own deliberations cannot well be other than one of cool benevolence. I hasten to add, however, that self-criticism such as this is far from binding one to any special tolerance towards dissentient opinions. It is perfectly legitimate to reject remorselessly theories which are contradicted by the very first steps in the analysis of observed facts, while yet being aware at the same time that the validity of one's own theory is only a provisional one.

We need not feel greatly disturbed in judging our speculation upon the life and death instincts by the fact that so many bewildering and obscure processes occur in it—such as one instinct being driven out by another or an instinct turning from the ego to an object, and so on. This is merely due to our being obliged to operate with scientific terms, that is to say with the figurative language peculiar to psychology (or, more precisely, to depth psychology). We could not otherwise describe the processes in question at all, and indeed we could not have become aware of them. The deficiencies in our description would probably vanish if we were already in a position to replace the psychological terms by physiological or chemical ones. It is true that they too are only part of a figurative language ; but it is one with which we have long been familiar and which is perhaps a simpler one as well.

On the other hand it should be made quite clear that the uncertainty of our speculation has been greatly increased by the necessity for borrowing from the science of biology. Biology is truly a land of unlimited possibilities. We may expect it to give us the most surprising information and we cannot guess what answers it will return in a few dozen years to the questions we have put to it. They may be of a kind which will blow away the whole of our artificial structure of hypotheses. If so, it may be asked why I have embarked upon such a line of thought as the present one, and in particular why I have decided to make it public. Well—I cannot deny that some of the analogies, correlations and connections which it contains seemed to me to deserve consideration.[55]

---

[55]I will add a few words to clarify our terminology, which has undergone some development in the course of the present

work. We came to know what the ' sexual instincts ' were from their relation to the sexes and to the reproductive function. We retained this name after we had been obliged by the findings of psycho-analysis to connect them less closely with reproduction. With the hypothesis of narcissistic libido and the extension of the concept of libido to the individual cells, the sexual instinct was transformed for us into Eros, which seeks to force together and hold together the portions of living substance. What are commonly called the sexual instincts are looked upon by us as the part of Eros which is directed towards objects. Our speculations have suggested that Eros operates from the beginning of life and appears as a ' life instinct ' in opposition to the ' death instinct ' which was brought into being by the coming to life of inorganic substance. These speculations seek to solve the riddle of life by supposing that these two instincts were struggling with each other from the very first. [Added 1921 :] It is not so easy, perhaps, to follow the transformations through which the concept of the ' ego instincts ' has passed. To begin with we applied that name to all the instinctual trends (of which we had no closer knowledge) which could be distinguished from the sexual instincts directed towards an object ; and we opposed the ego instincts to the sexual instincts of which the libido is the manifestation. Subsequently we came to closer grips with the analysis of the ego and recognized that a portion of the ' ego instincts ' is also of a libidinal character and has taken the subject's own ego as its object. These narcissistic self-preservative instincts had thenceforward to be counted among the libidinal sexual instincts. The opposition between the ego instincts and the sexual instincts was transformed into one between the ego instincts and the object instincts, both of a libidinal nature. But in its place a fresh opposition appeared between the libidinal (ego and object) instincts and others, which must be presumed to be present in the ego and which may perhaps actually be observed in the destructive instincts. Our speculations have transformed this opposition into one between the life instincts (Eros) and the death instincts.

VII

If it is really the case that seeking to restore an earlier state of things is such a universal characteristic of instincts, we need not be surprised that so many processes take place in mental life independently of the pleasure principle. This characteristic would be shared by all the component instincts and in their case would aim at returning once more to a particular stage in the course of development. These are matters over which the pleasure principle has as yet no control ; but it does not follow that any of them are necessarily opposed to it, and we have still to solve the problem of the relation of the instinctual processes of repetition to the dominance of the pleasure principle.

We have found that one of the earliest and most important functions of the mental apparatus is to 'bind' the instinctual impulses which impinge on it, to replace the primary process prevailing in them by the secondary process and to convert their mobile cathectic energy into a predominantly quiescent (tonic) cathexis. While this transformation is taking place no attention can be paid to the development of unpleasure ; but this does not imply the suspension of the pleasure principle. On the contrary, the transformation occurs in the service of the pleasure principle ; the binding is a preparatory act which introduces and assures the dominance of the pleasure principle.

Let us make a sharper distinction than we have hitherto made between function and tendency. The pleasure principle, then, is a tendency operating in the service of a function whose business it is to free the mental apparatus entirely from excitation or to keep the amount of excitation in it constant or to keep it as low as possible. We cannot yet decide with certainty in favour of any of these ways of putting it ; but it is clear that the function thus described would be concerned with the most universal endeavour of all living substance—namely to return to the quiescence of the inorganic world. We have all experienced how the greatest pleasure attainable by us, that of the sexual act, is associated with a momentary extinction of a highly intensified excitation. The binding of an instinctual impulse would be a preliminary function designed to prepare the excitation for its final elimination in the pleasure of discharge.

This raises the question of whether feelings of pleasure and unpleasure can be produced equally from bound and from unbound excitational processes. And there seems to be no doubt whatever that the unbound or primary processes give rise to far more intense feelings in both directions than the bound or secondary ones. Moreover the primary processes are the earlier in time ; at the beginning of mental life there are no others, and we may infer that if the pleasure principle had not already been operative in *them* it could never have been established for the later ones. We thus reach what is at bottom no very simple conclusion, namely that at the beginning of mental life the struggle for pleasure was far more intense than later but not so unrestricted : it had to submit to frequent interruptions. In later times the dominance of the pleasure principle is very much more secure, but it itself has no more escaped the process of taming than the other instincts in general. In any case, whatever it is that causes the appearance of feelings of pleasure and unpleasure in processes of excitation must be present in the secondary process just as it is in the primary one.

Here might be the starting-point for fresh investigations. Our consciousness communicates to us feelings from within not only of pleasure and unpleasure but also of a peculiar tension which in its turn can be either pleasurable or unpleasurable. Should the difference between these feelings enable us to distinguish between bound and unbound processes of energy ? or is the feeling of tension to be related to the absolute magnitude, or perhaps to the level, of the cathexis, while the pleasure and unpleasure series indicates a change in the magnitude of the cathexis *within a given unit of time* ? Another striking fact is that the life instincts have so much more contact with our internal perception—emerging as breakers of the peace and constantly producing tensions whose release is felt as pleasure—while the death instincts seem to do their work unobtrusively. The pleasure principle seems actually to serve the death instincts.

It is true that it keeps watch upon stimuli from
without, which are regarded as dangers by both
kinds of instincts ; but it is more especially on guard
against increases of stimulation from within, which
would make the task of living more difficult. This
in turn raises a host of other questions to which we
can at present find no answer. We must be patient
and await fresh methods and occasions of research.
We must be ready, too, to abandon a path that
we have followed for a time, if it seems to be leading
to no good end. Only believers, who demand that
science shall be a substitute for the catechism they
have given up, will blame an investigator for developing or even transforming his views. We may take
comfort, too, for the slow advances of our scientific
knowledge in the words of the poet :
' Was man nicht erfliegen kann, muss man erhinken.

. . . .

Die Schrift sagt, es ist keine Sünde zu hinken.'[56]

---

[56][' What we cannot reach flying we must reach limping
. . . . . The Book tells us it is no sin to limp.' The last lines of
' Die beiden Gulden,' a version by Rückert of one of the
Maqâmât of al-Hariri.]

LIST OF WORKS REFERRED TO
IN THE TEXT

[Titles of books and periodicals are in italics ; titles of pages are in inverted commas. Abbreviations are in accordance with the *World List of Scientific Periodicals* (Oxford, 1934). Numerals in thick type refer to volumes ; ordinary numerals refer to pages. *G.S.* = Freud, *Gesammelte Schriften*, Vienna, 1924-34 ; *G.W.* = Freud, *Gesammelte Werke*, London, 1940- ; *C.P.* = Freud *Collected Papers*, London, 1924-50.]

ADLER, A. (1908).—' Der Aggressionsbetrieb im Leben und in der Neurose,' *Fortschr. Med.*, No. 19.

BREUER, J. and FREUD, S. (1892).—' Zur Theorie des hysterischen Anfalls ', in FREUD, S., *G.W.*, **17,** 9.
    (*Trans.* : ' On the Theory of Hysterical Attacks,' in FREUD, S., *C.P.*, **5,** 27.)
  (1893).—' Über den psychischen Mechanismus hysterischer Phänomene,' in FREUD, S., *G.S.*, **1,** 7 ; *G.W.*, **1.**
    (*Trans.* : ' On the Psychical Mechanism of Hysterical Phenomena,' in FREUD, S., *C.P.*, **1,** 24.)
  (1895).—*Studien über Hysterie*, Vienna.
    (*Trans.* : *Studies in Hysteria*, New York, 1936.)

DOFLEIN, F. (1919).—*Das Problem des Todes und der Unsterblichkeit bei den Pflanzen und Tieren*, Jena.

FECHNER, G. T. (1873).—*Einige Ideen zur Schöpfungs- und Entwicklungsgeschichte der Organismen*, Leipzig.

FERENCZI, S. (1913).—' Entwicklungsstufen des Wirklichkeitssinnes,' *Int. Z. Psychoanal*, **1,** 124.
    (*Trans.* : ' Stages in the Development of the Sense of Reality,' *Contributions to Psycho-Analysis*, Boston, 1916, 213.)

Fliess, W. (1906).—*Der Ablauf des Lebens*, Vienna.

Freud, S. (1892).—' Brief an Josef Breuer,' *G.W.*, **17,** 5.
(*Trans.* : ' Letter to Josef Breuer,' *C.P.*, **5,** 25.)

(1900).—*Die Traumdeutung, G.S.*, **2** and **3** ; *G.W.*, **2** and **3.**
(*Trans.* : *The Interpretation of Dreams*, Revised ed., London, 1932.)

(1905).—*Drei Abhandlungen zur Sexualtheorie, G.S.*, **5,** 1 ; *G.W.*, **5,** 1.
(*Trans.* : *Three Essays on the Theory of Sexuality*, London, 1949.)

(1908).—' Die " kulturelle " Sexualmoral und die moderne Nervosität,' *G.S.*, **5,** 143 ; *G.W.*, **7,** 143.
(*Trans.* : ' " Civilized " Sexual Morality and Modern Nervousness,' *C.P.*, **2,** 76.)

(1914*a*).—' Zur Einführung des Narzissmus,' *G.S.*, **6,** 155 ; *G.W.*, **10,** 138.
(*Trans.* : ' On Narcissism : an Introduction,' *C.P.*, **4,** 30.)

(1914*b*).—' Weitere Ratschläge zur Technik der Psycho-analyse : Erinnern, Wiederholen und Durcharbeiten,' *G.S.*, **6,** 109 ; *G.W.*, **10,** 126.
(*Trans.* : ' Further Recommendations in the Technique of Psycho-Analysis : Recollection, Repetition and Working Through,' *C.P.*, **2,** 366.)

(1915*a*).—' Triebe und Triebschicksale,' *G.S.*, **5,** 443 ; *G.W.*, **10,** 210.
(*Trans.* : ' Instincts and their Vicissitudes,' *C.P.*, **4,** 60.)

(1915*b*).—' Das Unbewusste,' *G.S.*, **5,** 480 ; *G.W.*, **10,** 264.
(*Trans.* : ' The Unconscious,' *C.P.*, **4,** 98.)

(1916).—' Metapsychologische Ergänzung zur Traumlehre,' *G.S.*, **5,** 520 ; *G.W.*, **10,** 412.
(*Trans.* : ' Metapsychological Supplement to the Theory of Dreams,' *C.P.*, **4,** 137.)

(1917).—' Eine Kindheitserinnerung aus " Dichtung und Wahrheit " ', *G.S.*, **10,** 357 ; *G.W.*, **12,** 14.

(*Trans.* : ' A Childhood Recollection from " *Dichtung und Wahrheit* ",' *C.P.*, **4,** 357.)

(1919).—Einleitung zu *Zur Psychoanalyse der Kriegsneurosen*, *G.S.*, **11,** 252 ; *G.W.*, **12,** 327. (See FREUD, S., FERENCZI, S., etc., 1919.)

(*Trans.* : Preface to *Psycho-Analysis and the War Neuroses*, *C.P.*, **5,** 83.)

(1923).—' Bemerkungen zur Theorie und Praxis der Traumdeutung,' *G.S.*, **3,** 305 ; *G.W.*, **13,** 301.

(*Trans.* : ' Remarks upon the Theory and Practice of Dream-Interpretation,' *C.P.*, **5,** 136.)

(1925).—' Notiz über den " Wunderblock " ', *G.S.*, **6,** 415 ; *G.W.*, **14,** 3.

(*Trans.* : 'A Note upon the " Mystic Writing-Pad " ', *C.P.*, **5,** 175.)

FREUD, S., FERENCZI, S., ABRAHAM, K., SIMMEL, E. and JONES, E. (1919).—*Zur Psychoanalyse der Kriegsneurosen*, Vienna. (See FREUD, S., 1919.)

(*Trans.* : *Psycho-Analysis and the War Neuroses*, London, 1921.)

GOETTE, A. (1883).—*Über den Ursprung des Todes*, Hamburg.

HARTMANN, M. (1906).—*Tod und Fortpflanzung*, Munich.

JUNG, C. G. (1909).—' Die Bedeutung des Vaters für das Schicksal des Einzelnen,' *Jb. psychoanal. psychopath. Forsch.*, **1,** 155.

(*Trans.* : 'The Significance of the Father in the Destiny of the Individual,' *Collected Papers on Analytical Psychology*, London, 1916, 156.)

LIPSCHÜTZ, A. (1914).—*Warum wir streben*, Stuttgart.

LOW, B. (1920).—*Psycho-Analysis*, London.

MARCINOWSKI, J. (1918).—' Die erotischen Quellen der Minderwertigkeitsgefühle,' *Z. Sexualwiss*, **4,** 313.

PFEIFER, S. (1919).—' Äusserungen infantil-erotischer Triebe in Spiele,' *Imago*, **5,** 243.

RANK, O.—(1907).—*Der Künstler*, Vienna.

SCHOPENHAUER, A. (1851).—' Über die anscheinende Absichtlichkeit im Schicksale des Einzelnen,' *Parerga und Paralipomena*, **1,** (*Sämtliche Werke*, ed. Hübscher, Leipzig, 1938, **5,** 213).

SPIELREIN, S. (1912).—' Die Destruktion als Ursache des Werdens,' *Jb. psychoanal. psychopath. Forsch.*, **4,** 465.

STÄRCKE, A. (1914).—Introduction to Dutch translation of FREUD, S., 1908, Leyden.

WEISMANN, A. (1882).—*Über die Dauer des Lebens*, Jena.
(1884).—*Über Leben und Tod*, Jena.
(1892).—*Das Keimplasma*, Jena.
  (*Trans.* : The Germ-Plasm, London, 1893.)

ZIEGLER, K. (1913).—' Menschen- und Weltenwerden,' *Neue Jb. klass. Altert.*, **31,** 529.

INDEX

Abraham, K., 9.

Adler, A., 72.

Ambivalence, 73, 74.

Anticathexis, 36.

Anxiety, 10.

Breuer, J., 4, 11, 28, 31, 37, 44.

Calkins, 64.

Cathexis—
  and trauma, 39.
  Breuer's mobile, 44.
  bound, 31, 36, 38, 44, 85.
  freely flowing, 38.

Compulsion to repeat—
  and children's play, 25.
  and dreams, 25, 40.
  and ego instincts, 58, 59.
  and regressive character of
    instincts, 81.
  in analysis, 19, 21, 23, 46.
  in normal people, 23, 24.
  instinctual character of, 25,
    45, 46.
  related to pleasure principle,
    21.

Consciousness—
  and memory traces, 29.
  and system Pcpt.-Cs., 28, 29.
  origin of, 29, 31.
  perceptual, 27.
  seat of, 28.

Constancy principle, 4.

Cs. system, 27, 29-31, 34.

Darwin, C., 77.

Death—
  from internal causes, 59,
    60, 62.
  instincts, 51, 53, 59, 61-63,
    66, 67, 72-74, 76, 78, 84,
    87.
  the goal of life, 50.
  Weismann's theory, 60-62.

Dementia præcox, 42.

Development—
  organic, 52, 55.
  impulse towards higher, 55.

Doflein, F., 63.

Dreams—
  anxiety, 39, 40.

93

our
generation.

This is Ginger's story.

GINGER ™

HOME AWAY FROM HOME

BY

CYNTHIA HAIGH

ILLUSTRATED BY TRISH ROUELLE

An Our Generation® *book*

MAISON JOSEPH BATTAT LTD. *Publisher*

A very special thanks to the editor,
Joanne Burke Casey and
to Susan Love.

Our Generation® Books is a registered trademark of Maison Joseph Battat Ltd.
Text copyright © 2014 by Cynthia Haigh
ISBN: 978-0-9891839-7-0
Printed in China

For my sweet little June

Read all the adventures in the
Our Generation® Book Series

Read more about **Our Generation®** books and dolls online:
www.ogdolls.com

CONTENTS

EXTRA! EXTRA! READ ALL ABOUT IT!
*Big words, wacky words, powerful words, funny words...
what do they all mean? They are marked with this symbol *.
Look them up in the Glossary at the end of this book.*

Chapter One

NO PLACE LIKE HOME

The Christmas holidays were almost here—my very, very favorite time of the year. So why was I standing alone in the middle of my bedroom, close to having a full-blown hissy fit?

And why was I staring at my pink polka-dotted suitcase with the bright green bow that was jammed so full I couldn't zip it closed all the way? Not even after I had sat and bounced on it a few times while no one was looking!

Tomorrow morning, my mom and dad, my grandmother (whom I call "Mormor"), my Aunt Holly and I were leaving our home in Chicago to fly thousands of miles across the Atlantic Ocean to another country.

The plan was to visit the rest of my family

on my mom's side. I had never met those members of our family except for my Aunt Ingrid, who had come to visit us a couple of times.

They live in Sweden, which is in northern Europe in an area called Scandinavia. I should have been incredibly excited to visit another country and meet my relatives for the first time. Instead, there I was, gritting my teeth and just about one step away from stomping my feet in total frustration*.

I had to try to control myself. Mormor was across the hall in the guest room and she would not like to see me acting that way. She would describe it as "unbecoming."

Mormor is the greatest grandmother *in the whole wide world*. She is kind, caring, generous and patient. I think she may also be one of the smartest grandmothers *in the whole wide world*. She has taught me so many things.

I could go on and on about how great my grandmother is. All I know is, when I grow up I want to be just like her.

She would have been upset to see me behave this way because she happens to think that I'm one of the best granddaughters *in the whole wide world*! I have a reputation* to live up to and the last thing I'd want to do is disappoint her. Behaving in a positive way is important to Mormor and I always want her to be proud of me.

So I took a deep breath, counted to five and tried to relax. Only then could I calmly look at the piece of paper I clutched in my hand: "Ginger's List of Things to Bring."

It was a list of all the items I wanted to pack. I had placed a check mark next to those items I had already stuffed in my overflowing suitcase.

Mom said it was way too full. But how was I to leave home for a faraway country without all my special holiday mementos*?

How could I leave behind the woven-paper heart baskets that Aunt Holly and I had made last year? Or the stockings she had shown me how to embroider*? Or my special ball ornament that was covered in pink glitter and tied with a striped ribbon bow? Mormor gave that to me on my very first Christmas. Since then it has been hung on the tree every holiday.

Without all my special holiday treasures we may as well just cross Christmas off the calendar, I thought with a sigh.

There were so many things I just *had* to pack. Like the gnome ornament that Aunt

Holly had given me. That cute little fellow with his pointy hat and soft white beard spent most of his time on our Christmas tree. For extra fun, we would place him in different poses and include him in our family holiday photos.

One of my favorite pictures shows "Nutmeg Gnome" sitting with us around the table during our Christmas Eve meal. In another, he's hanging on the Christmas tree, looking as though he's munching on the garland of popcorn and cranberries we had strung around it.

That got me wondering if I needed to bring popcorn and cranberries... *Gee, do they even know what a cranberry is in Sweden? And what if they think it's silly to hang food on the Christmas tree?*

But what was really getting to me and what I was most upset and sad about was the one thing I knew I'd never be able to pack— Mr. Snuggles, my precious rabbit.

A little over a year ago, on the morning of Halloween, I peered out the window and spied a fluffy, black-and-white rabbit at the foot of our steps. Mom and I had put out a big bale of hay with some jack-o'-lanterns for Halloween night. There sat a little rabbit, chomping away at our decorations!

When I opened the door, he immediately stopped chewing the hay and froze completely still. He looked at me as if to say, "What's the matter? I'm not doing anything wrong."

Mr. Snuggles has big floppy ears. He's also a wee bit chubby. Judging from his looks, my mom said he wasn't a wild rabbit. He was a domesticated rabbit. Mom explained that this meant he was tame, and used to being around people. She figured he was someone's lost pet.

Mom called our local animal shelter* and they took all the information about him.

In the meantime, one of my best friends, Caroline, and I made a "FOUND RABBIT"

flier. After we took a picture of Mr. Snuggles we pasted it on paper and included our phone number. We drew some bright orange carrots around the edges of the paper. It looked really eye-catching so we decided to make lots of copies.

Dad went along and helped us hang the fliers in stores and around the area where we lived. People seemed to be very curious and many gathered in front of the signs as soon as we posted them. Some people told us they would even walk around their own neighborhoods and check to make sure nobody's rabbit got out and was missing.

Weeks passed and no one ever contacted the animal shelter or us about a lost rabbit. I never told anyone, but I was secretly happy that no one claimed him. By that time we had become very attached to Mr. Snuggles.

Dad and I had spent many hours making him his own house. Dad called it "The Bunny Bungalow*." His house was just like a real bungalow except it had hay covering the entire floor!

Every day after I got home from school he would immediately hop out of his little "bungalow" to see me. Whenever I sat down he'd jump up on my lap and cuddle there for as long as I let him stay.

Not only were we attached to him, but he was attached to us! Mr. Snuggles, our little snugglebunny, had become an important member of our family.

Now we were getting ready to leave Mr. Snuggles for the first time. Caroline was going to take care of him. I hoped that he wouldn't think I was abandoning* him.

I was going to miss him so much.

Chapter Two

THE WARM WELCOME

That night, Caroline and her mom came over to our home so we could go over the instructions for the care of Mr. Snuggles. If there was anyone else who cared about him as much as I did, it was Caroline.

I knew that he couldn't be in better hands. Caroline always amazes me because she is the most responsible person *in the whole wide world*. If you want to get something done right, Caroline is the one to go to.

Ms. O'Leary, our teacher, has called her "Conscientious Caroline." She knew that if she used that particular word to describe Caroline we would learn that it means to be trustworthy and always careful to do the right thing.

Ms. O'Leary said that if a person's picture

was used in a dictionary to describe a trait*, a picture of Caroline would be there right next to the word "conscientious"!

As Caroline and her mom were leaving, I gave them a box of the flower-shaped Ginger Wish Cookies my mom and I had baked that morning. We have a tradition* of baking Ginger Wish Cookies during the holiday season.

Every year it's part of that tradition to give a box to each of my best friends, Caroline, Jenny and Megan. We always get together so that we can make a "ginger wish."

We each hold a cookie in the palm of one hand and think of a secret wish. And then, with the index* finger of our other hand, we tap the cookie in the middle. Whoever cracks her cookie into three pieces has her wish come true.

Last year, all four of us cracked each of our cookies in three pieces. Imagine that—all of our wishes were going to come true!

Because I wouldn't be home for the holiday this year, we pinky-swore that we would make our ginger wish at 8:00 p.m. on Tuesday night, two days after I would arrive in Sweden. Even though we couldn't *be* together, we would be doing the same *thing* together.

My mom and dad peeked into my room to remind me that it was almost bedtime and I needed to get up early for our flight to Sweden the next morning.

Mom suggested that I wrap up the ginger cookies in foil and place the heart baskets in a cardboard folder. She said I should pack them last since they were to go in my polka-dotted travel case, which I was carrying on the plane.

I decided I'd leave them on the counter and pack them in the morning. They would just fit on top of all the tissue paper that was rolled up to protect my special pink glitter ball ornament that Mom agreed to let me bring.

It was really hard for me to sleep because I wasn't looking forward to the long, boring flight ahead. I was disappointed about not having a traditional Christmas here in Chicago and I was feeling blue* about missing Mr. Snuggles so much.

And I was really, *really* anxious* about meeting my cousins for the first time. *What if we don't have anything in common?* I wondered. *Even worse, what if we don't like each other?*

✿ ✿

Morning arrived. Mom must have been so tired tending to all the last-minute details the night before that she set the alarm wrong. Instead of entering 5:30 *a.m.* the alarm was set for 5:30 *p.m.*

It was a good thing I was restless and couldn't sleep that well because I awoke earlier than usual at 6:00 a.m.

We had to rush around and gather up our things. My mom and dad grabbed our plane tickets and we practically flew out the door. I barely had enough time to give Mr. Snuggles a big kiss and a hug.

Wouldn't you know the traffic was backed up for miles on our way to the airport?!

My dad is always calm and nothing ever seems to get him upset. Everyone likes to say that he's as "cool as a cucumber." Well, even *he* was getting nervous that we would be late. He was actually talking to himself!

I wondered if there was an expression "as warm as a pepper," or something like that. I sure could have used one to describe my dad when his face was getting all red and he was mumbling under his breath the entire ride!

Fortunately, we arrived at the airport just in the nick of time. The airport terminal was all decked out in fancy decorations and sparkling lights. Aunt Holly remarked how festive* everything looked.

But I couldn't help notice *all the people*—they were *everywhere*. The whole airport was bustling* with everyone rushing to get to their flights on time. There were long lines and many people looked worn out and tired.

There were college students with big backpacks. They looked happy to be heading home. I saw grandparents carrying gifts and families with children and babies in strollers.

I wondered if they were excited to be getting away for the holidays. Or were they like me? Were they nervous about where they were going? Were they unhappy not to be home for the holidays?

22

We waited in the security line for what seemed like a year. I was so excited when we finally boarded the plane. I sat next to Mormor.

After the plane took off, Mormor and I did some word puzzles, which was a lot of fun. And she shared some family history that I didn't know about how our ancestors* immigrated* to America from Sweden.

"That's why you call me 'Mormor.' It is a Swedish word for your grandmother on your mother's side. I always called my grandmother 'Mormor' and I called my grandmother on my father's side 'Farmor.' I wanted to follow that tradition with you and your cousins," she explained.

She continued on, telling me how her grandparents and her great-grandparents came to America in the late 1800s.

I was really curious to know why they left their homes to go live in another country.

"At that time, there weren't enough jobs in Sweden for everyone," Mormor said. "They came to America where there were lots of jobs and they felt they'd have a better life."

Many of the immigrants were farmers so they moved to places where there was plenty of farmland. Illinois was one of those places.

After a generation* or two, many Swedish-Americans moved to the city. Chicago had more Swedish-Americans than any other city in the United States.

I thought about how worried I was, leaving my home to spend the holidays in Sweden. *Some of those people were leaving their homes forever.* Boy, did I feel a little silly.

All of those people were going to a strange country with a strange language and I was upset about going to Sweden for less than *two weeks*!

I wondered why my aunt Ingrid lived in Sweden instead of America. Mormor smiled. "Back when your aunt was going to college in Chicago, she met this nice young man who happened to be studying in the United States.

He was from Sweden."

They began dating and then they fell in love. Aunt Ingrid went to visit him in Sweden and she loved it there. That "nice young man" became my uncle Max. After they got married, they ended up living near Stockholm, which is the capital of Sweden and its largest city.

"How did he know English?" I asked.

Mormor said most Swedes speak English. All students start to learn English in third grade.

Mormor and I started getting sleepy.

I decided to read a chapter from one of my books about a girl who experiences life as one fun adventure after another. I giggled out loud when I read how she would sleep backwards in her bed.

I may be adventurous and try something different like that, I thought. *Or maybe I'll even wear my pajamas backwards!*

After a while I fell asleep, which made the long flight seem to go by much faster. I woke up to the sound of the pilot announcing that we would be landing shortly.

The pilot told us what the time was in Sweden since their time is seven hours ahead of our time in Chicago. He described the weather as being somewhat cold with snow expected.

The plane landed smoothly and it took some time to collect our luggage, but we made it out the door at last!

Standing there, in a roped-off area, were Aunt Ingrid, Uncle Max and my cousins, Brigitta and Hans. They looked a little older than they did in the last pictures that had been sent to us. Brigitta is older than I am by a little more than a year and Hans is younger than I am.

Aunt Ingrid and Uncle Max were holding a welcoming banner that was hand-written:

Mormor, Aunt Astrid, Aunt Holly,
Uncle Rob and Ginger—
Welcome to Sweden with all our love!

Brigitta also held up a smaller sign that read:

Thank You for Visiting Us, Cousin Ginger!

It had a border of red hearts. Gosh, those signs made me feel so much better.

I happened to notice that Hans stood behind the others with his hands in his coat pockets. It seemed strange that he was the only one not holding a sign.

The adults started happily shrieking and then hugging and kissing. My aunt and uncle kissed each of us, first on one side of our face and then on the opposite side. My dad had told me earlier that this is the custom in Europe.

Aunt Ingrid wrapped her arms around me so tight that I thought I would crack in half. Actually I was thinking I was going to crack in three pieces—just like a *ginger cookie!*

Chapter Three

A COMMON BOND

Brigitta had a smile as big as Lake Michigan. "I have never been *so* excited in all my life! I am *so* happy we finally got to meet each other. I have waited *so* long for this occasion!" she exclaimed, as she jumped up and down.

Hans was another matter. He looked at me and then he looked down at his shoes. Aunt Ingrid gently poked Hans, "Say hello to your cousin Ginger."

"Hello," he said, without looking up.

It's a good thing Brigitta seems so happy to be meeting me, I thought, *because Hans sure doesn't seem thrilled.*

We left the airport and Aunt Ingrid and Uncle Max were each driving a car. I was relieved to learn that the girls were to travel in one car and the boys in another.

It was fun to look out the window and see all the different houses. Many had very tall roofs. Some had wood planks going up and down instead of rows of wood going side to side. A lot of the houses were painted interesting colors, and most were not at all like the houses in my neighborhood back home in Chicago.

When we arrived at my aunt and uncle's house, it looked like something out of a storybook. My mom called it charming. It was red with black trim and had two chimneys. Hanging on the door was a large green wreath, dotted with pinecones and tied with a red bow.

We walked inside, and draped across the fireplace was another big banner that said "*God Jul!*" which is Swedish for Merry Christmas. In the corner of the room stood a tall, beautiful Christmas tree. Uncle Max said it was a spruce, a tree that grows in many parts of Sweden. It reminded me of the Christmas trees we have at home, and that made me feel a little homesick.

The tree was decorated with ornaments of animals that were made out of straw. Also hanging on the branches were the most delicious-looking candy and treats, which I learned Brigitta and Hans had helped make.

I laughed to myself when I saw it. To think I was worried that they would view me as weird because I placed garlands of popcorn and cranberries on our Christmas tree *while theirs*

was almost completely covered with food!

We all sat down to talk and enjoy some warm drinks. All of us, that is, except for Hans. He quickly retreated* upstairs to his bedroom. I think he may have resented* us for spoiling his Christmas. Well, at least Hans and I had something in common because my Christmas wasn't going to be the same either!

After a while, Brigitta brought me upstairs to show me her bedroom. It was a large room that was very bright and cheerful. Two matching white beds were covered with pretty purple-flowered comforters and puffy pillows. A shaggy rug was on the floor.

Brigitta and I had many things to talk about. We found out that we have a lot in common, especially when it comes to collecting.

Brigitta loves dogs. She has a shelf full of dog statues. In fact, just about anything with a dog on it has made it into her collection.

I also noticed several Dala horses on her nightstand. They are small wooden horses, painted with bright designs and colors.

But the thing that is really amazing and coincidental* is that we both collect snow globes! *What are the chances of that?* I thought.

Brigitta has a few snow globes with Christmas scenes. One is a Christmas tree coated in snow and another shows skaters on a frozen pond. A musical globe of a sleigh plays a holiday song when it's wound up.

It was getting late, so Brigitta and I decided to get some sleep. While she changed into her plaid nightgown, I pulled my favorite pajamas that have bunnies, foxes, owls and bears on them out of my suitcase and set my small travel case aside. I figured I could unpack everything else the next morning.

Brigitta plopped down on her bed and said, "Ginger, kick your feet up and relax."

I immediately put my head at the bottom of the bed and my feet up on the pillow. Brigitta laughed so hard.

"Is this how you all sleep in America?"

she asked.

"No," I answered, "I got the idea from a book I read about a girl who always slept that way so she could wiggle her toes."

"Good night, Ginger, sweet dreams," she said. Brigitta giggled as she turned off the light.

"And sweet dreams to you, Brigitta."

What a difference one night made. Instead of being nervous and worried I was starting to feel a little more relaxed and happy to have made the trip.

Looking back to the previous night, all I could think was *am I ever glad I didn't have that hissy fit. What a silly scene that would have been!*

The next morning I woke up refreshed from a good night's sleep. Brigitta had gotten up a little earlier and gone downstairs to help get breakfast ready.

Even though it was late, the adults were still sitting around the kitchen table in their robes and slippers. They were drinking coffee, reminiscing* and laughing about old times.

Hans was listening to their conversation but he quickly got up, tucked his chair under the table and dashed upstairs.

Gosh! I thought sourly. *What's up with him?*

Chapter Four
RECIPE FOR DISASTER

The table was covered with a cheery red-and-green tablecloth and several different kinds of food that I had never seen served for breakfast. Brigitta was eating an open-faced sandwich. It consisted of one slice of dark wheat bread with a creamy spread and some cucumbers on top!

For a moment I wondered if I had overslept longer than I thought and that it was really lunchtime. Brigitta assured me it was still breakfast time and explained that open-faced sandwiches are a typical breakfast in Sweden.

A pretty basket held the most yummy-looking buns that were filled with almond paste and a type of red jam I had never had before. Next to that was a large platter overflowing with delicious fresh fruit. Some of the berries on it looked like tiny strawberries.

Something that did look familiar was the cereal. It was muesli, which we also eat at home and is similar to granola. It's made from oats, nuts and dried fruit.

Brigitta made me a sandwich out of a whole-grain cracker with orange marmalade on top, and then I had some muesli and fruit. *I know one thing,* I thought. *There's so much food I'll never have to worry about going hungry or my stomach growling!*

After breakfast, Brigitta and I went upstairs and I began to unpack, since I had been way too tired to do it the night before. I decided I'd start by unwrapping the Ginger Wish Cookies and the heart baskets.

All of a sudden I got a sinking feeling. They were not in my polka-dotted travel case. "Oh no!" I shouted. "I forgot to pack them!

I must have left them on the counter in my rush to leave quickly so we wouldn't miss our flight."

Brigitta assured me that things would be fine. "Don't worry, Ginger. We can make heart baskets and even bake some more ginger cookies, too."

She quickly ran downstairs and came back up with a heart basket that she had made with her mom, dad and Hans.

"They're easy to make," said Brigitta. "We can do it together."

Even though I figured it would never be as special as the ones I forgot to bring, since I had made mine with Aunt Holly, it would be fun to make a heart basket with my cousin.

Brigitta was very ambitious* because she also wanted to make a batch of Ginger Wish Cookies. She told me that she and Hans make cookies like them every year. They are traditional cookies in Sweden, called "*pepparkakor*."

We hurried back downstairs and asked my mom for a list of all the ingredients.

As I read it out loud, Brigitta looked in the

cabinet to make sure we had everything.

I would say "flour" and she would say, "check." And then I'd say "sugar" and she'd say, "sugar, check." When I finally got to the bottom of the list, the last ingredient I rattled off was "ginger." After a few moments she pulled out a spice jar filled with ginger and said, "check." We both happily squealed, "Yay!"

We had every ingredient from the recipe. Now we could make Ginger Wish Cookies!

We both began measuring everything and putting all of it in order on the counter. Brigitta read the directions and I followed them.

In between we chatted about all sorts of things, like our hobbies, friends, school, music and movies. And of course we had to talk about our prized possessions—our snow globes.

The cookie dough was finally mixed and we began to roll it out. As we used cookie cutters to cut out the shapes it seemed a little gooey. We figured that after baking, the cookies would become crisp and golden.

My mom helped place the cookie sheet in the oven and we set the timer for nine minutes.

After a few minutes we could smell them, and what a delicious smell it was! We could hardly wait till the timer rang.

Bing bing bing went the timer and we both jumped up so fast we knocked one of the chairs over. Aunt Ingrid helped take the cookies out of the oven.

"*Oh no!*" I yelped.

"*Oh no, no, no,*" moaned Brigitta.

We couldn't believe what we saw.

Chapter Five

TIME IS NOT ON MY SIDE

There in front of us, looking like one gooey glob, was the biggest, soggiest-looking cookie *in the whole wide world*!

Our first attempt at making Ginger Wish Cookies was a disaster. How could we have goofed up the recipe?

Meanwhile, Aunt Holly giggled as she quickly grabbed her camera to photograph it.

"What about our wish?" I frantically asked. "I pinky-swore with my friends that we would crack our ginger cookies tonight at eight o'clock. Not only can I not break my promise, but it would be terrible to break a tradition that we've had together for so long."

"Don't worry, Ginger. We have enough ingredients to start another batch," Brigitta said, trying to comfort me.

Almost in unison* we declared that this time we would *really really* concentrate on mixing the exact amounts of the recipe.

So once again we mixed the ingredients. We were much more careful. We checked and double-checked that we were following the recipe to a "T"*.

And then we waited.

In the meantime, Aunt Holly showed us the photo she had printed out. She called it "The Largest Ginger Cookie in the Whole Wide World," since she says that seems to be my favorite expression!

Bing bing bing went the timer—the nine minutes were up. We held our breath as Aunt Ingrid opened the oven door. This time we looked at piping hot, crisp, golden cookies.

They were delicious-looking and perfectly formed. We set them aside to cool and I must say, it sure was tempting to pop a couple in our mouths. But we knew better.

I discovered just how talented Brigitta is. She is very artistic and loves doing arts and crafts projects. She brought out several boxes filled to the brim with supplies, including paper, paint and sparkles.

"My mom, dad, Hans and I love to make things," said Brigitta excitedly.

"Yes, I can see that," I said, "There's enough stuff in those boxes to build another Eiffel Tower!"

Just seeing all the different materials made me want to create something but I wasn't sure exactly what it would be. Right then Brigitta said, "I have an idea. We have enough stuff to make snowflakes for the Snowflake Ball."

"What's the Snowflake Ball?" I asked.

"It's a big party held downtown at the Art and Music Center," Brigitta explained. "We go every year. Everyone who buys a ticket to get in can bring a homemade snowflake. There's a contest with different categories like funniest snowflake, coldest-looking, most beautiful and most unusual.

"Last year my dad won a ribbon for "The Fastest-melting Snowflake." He put together a huge snowflake wearing a hula skirt with a sunbeam shining down on it."

"That sounds like it should have also won the funniest category," I laughed.

Brigitta went on to tell me that all the money from the sale of tickets goes to the Art and Music Center, which offers art and music classes for everyone, children as well as adults.

We began making snowflakes. Brigitta was so creative. I tried, but I was no match for her.

I ended up with a snowflake that looked like a hexagon-shaped plate. Since it looked just like the six-sided white dinner plates we eat off of every night at home, I thought I'd put some food on it and call it "The Hungry Snowflake."

"Wow, that's great, Ginger, and *so* imaginative," Brigitta said enthusiastically*.

That was enough to make me feel proud. *My cousin, Brigitta, probably one of the most artistic and creative girls in the whole wide world, is telling me how great my snowflake is!*

We carefully wrapped up our snowflakes and put them aside. The next night was the Snowflake Ball and we were ready!

We had just finished dinner. Hans, Brigitta and I were helping to clean up and wash the dishes. All of a sudden I panicked*. "What time is it?" I asked. "I have to make sure I crack my Ginger Wish Cookie at exactly 8:00 p.m.!"

"It's 8:10," said Hans.

"Oh no!" I yelled. "This can't be—I was supposed to be cracking my ginger cookie ten minutes ago! I made a promise to my friends that we would all crack our cookies and make a wish at the exact same time!"

I slumped onto the kitchen chair with my head in my hands. *How could this have happened?* I thought. *I miss my friends. I miss my home. I miss Mr. Snuggles. And I've missed my opportunity to crack my cookie with Caroline, Jenny and Megan!*

"If it makes you feel any better, they haven't cracked their cookies either," Hans said coolly.

I was puzzled. "What do you mean?"

"Well, we're in a different time zone,"

Hans replied. "We are seven hours ahead of Chicago. That means it's only 1:10 in the afternoon there. So your friends haven't cracked their cookies yet."

"Wow, thanks Hans. I never even thought of that," I said.

"The reason I thought of it right away is that I did a school project on time zones. I found out a lot of things…like how the earth rotates slowly. And that any time the sun is directly above us it means it's noon where we are.

"But when it's noon here it's midnight someplace else. Someplace else happens to be halfway around the world from us," he said.

He explained that the world is divided up into 24 different time zones. Each zone is one hour apart. So if we are traveling east, it's one hour later each time we cross a time zone. If we go west, it would be one hour earlier each time.

I got to thinking not just about time zones, but about how well Hans explained it all to me. He didn't come off as a know-it-all and he certainly didn't make me feel stupid. This was a side of Hans I hadn't seen since we met.

Since we were talking about zones, I guess you could say this was a whole different zone he was in. Not his usual "be-by-myself" zone where he seemed to just want to get away and not be around me.

I realized there were important things to decide. *Should I set my alarm so that I'll get up and be cracking my ginger cookie when it's 8:00 p.m. in Chicago? That would mean I'd have to get up before 3:00 in the morning!*

There was only one answer. After all, I had made a promise and I, Ginger, trustworthy and responsible citizen* of the great Windy City of Chicago, keep my promises.

Chapter Six

A PROMISE IS A PROMISE

I began to think more about my plan. *Would it be rude to sneak downstairs in the middle of the night? Should I ask Aunt Ingrid and Uncle Max and my mom and dad ahead of time? Maybe I should ask Brigitta what I should do.*

Once we got upstairs I decided to tell Brigitta all about my plan.

"Wow, that sounds fun, Ginger," she said. "I know that this is a special tradition you have with your friends, but do you think I can do it with you? Do you think I can crack a Ginger Wish Cookie, too?"

At that moment I thought how great it was that my cousin Brigitta wanted to take part in my tradition. I had begun to think of her as one of the best cousins *in the whole wide world* and now she wanted to be included in my plan.

"I would love it if you did, Brigitta, but I think we better let your mom and dad know that we'll be sneaking down into the kitchen at night," I said.

"Yes, maybe you're right, Ginger," Brigitta agreed. "Let's go tell them now what we plan to do," Brigitta said.

"On second thought, Brigitta, I think we need to *ask* them if what we want to do is all right," I stated.

"OK, then let's go downstairs now and get it over with," she replied.

We both went downstairs to find everyone still sitting around and cheerfully chatting. Brigitta was the one who first broached* the subject with her parents.

Their reply was that we both really needed our sleep and it was just *too late* at night or *too early* in the morning, depending on how one was to look at it.

Mormor piped up, "Oh let them do it. It's important to them and Brigitta will now be able to participate in Ginger's tradition, too. It's only taking place this one time. If they're really tired they can sleep later."

Mormor understood that it is a tradition that I hold close to my heart.

"All right, you both can do it, but you must not make a lot of noise," said Aunt Ingrid.

"And I really think you both need some supervision at that time of night," my mom said softly as she pulled me aside.

Aunt Holly overheard what Mom said.

"Girls, just wake me up. What you're doing sounds like a lot of fun. After all, when will I ever get a chance to crack a ginger cookie and make a wish at three o'clock in the morning?" Aunt Holly laughed.

"And besides, I haven't had an adventure like this in a long time."

Brigitta and I were thrilled. We thought of our parents as being a bit strict so it was always great to have Aunt Holly around to liven things up. We were excited that she was going to be a part of the Ginger Wish Cookie tradition.

Brigitta and I rushed upstairs to set our alarm. We quickly changed into our pajamas and jumped into our cozy, warm beds. We had important business to tend to and we needed our rest!

Suddenly I was jolted out of a sound sleep…

COCKADOODLE-DOO!

"What?!" I gasped, as I popped up in my bed. "Brigitta! Wake up! There's a rooster in your house!"

COCKADOODLE-DOO!

Chapter Seven

NIGHTTIME ADVENTURE

"No," Brigitta said in a sleepy voice as she pressed the button on the alarm clock. "There's a Hans in my house and he played a little trick on us," she explained.

"You can set this to make animal noises, bells, and even songs. I guess Hans thought that since we were getting up so early, he'd put on the animal that wakes us up at sunrise."

That Hans is full of surprises, I thought. I rubbed my eyes and looked at the glowing numbers on the clock. 2:50 a.m.!

We quietly slid out of bed and crept into Aunt Holly's bedroom. There she stood, all ready for her "adventure."

The three of us tiptoed downstairs and into the kitchen.

We spotted the cookie jar on the table. I lifted off the lid and we each reached in for one.

Aunt Holly spoke about the memories she had of when she was a young girl. She and Aunt Ingrid, my mom and Mormor would make ginger cookies every holiday.

Before bedtime, they would crack the cookies and make a wish at the same time. Aunt Holly remembered how much fun it was for all of them, and especially how much my mother loved the tradition.

Brigitta didn't realize how I got my name so Aunt Holly explained why my mom named me "Ginger." She told her that it was to remind my mom of those fond holiday memories when they were all together.

Aunt Holly suddenly declared there was just a minute to go until three o'clock so we all had to get in "position" to crack our cookies.

"Remember," I said, "if it breaks in three pieces your wish will come true."

"Are we all ready?" asked Aunt Holly.

"Yes!" we both responded.

"Ready, set, go," I said in a very urgent but hushed voice.

Each of us opened our palms. Aunt Holly had three pieces. Brigitta had three pieces.

"Oh no!" I said as I began to count. "One, two, three, four, five pieces!" I groaned.

"Ginger, I think you were just being overly enthusiastic," said Aunt Holly tenderly.

"Oh well," I said. "I guess getting my wish this year is no big deal."

Deep down inside I knew it was. I didn't want them to know how disappointed I was.

After all, I didn't want to ruin it for them. I was *so* glad that Aunt Holly got to join us and make her wish after not doing it for all those years. And I was really pleased that Brigitta got her wish the very first time we tried it together.

Aunt Holly suggested we all head upstairs and get back into our warm beds.

"It's early morning and we still have a lot to do in preparation for the holidays," she said.

The three of us hugged each other. This time we each tiptoed *up* the stairs. When we got to the top landing Aunt Holly whispered, "Goodnight girls, and thank you for letting me be part of this. I really enjoyed sharing those special moments with you."

She kissed us both on our foreheads and went into her room.

Brigitta and I quietly got into bed. Just after Brigitta turned off her light she asked somewhat hesitantly, "Ginger, do you really think that wishes come true?"

"I don't know how it works for everyone else, but I know that every time my friends and I cracked our ginger cookies our wishes came true," I assured her.

"That's good," she said, "and thanks for letting me be part of it, too. I'm *so* glad you're my cousin. Tonight was exciting—I never got to do anything like that before."

"Even though I won't get my wish, it was fun for me, too," I said. "Not only did I get to keep my promise to my friends, but I got an added bonus of sharing this tradition with you and Aunt Holly."

"Goodnight, Ginger, see you in the morning," said Brigitta.

"Goodnight, Brigitta," I answered.

I rolled over and thought about a lot of things. *Were Caroline, Jenny and Megan able to crack their cookies in three pieces? Did they do it at exactly the moment we did? Are they going to get their wishes? And would I be able to get over the fact that I wouldn't get my wish?*

There was so much to think about, yet I was getting so sleepy.

I knew we had another busy day ahead of us. The Snowflake Ball was taking place that night and I could hardly wait!

Chapter Eight

TINGLING WITH CHRISTMAS SPIRIT

Brigitta and I must have been very tired because we sure did sleep late. We discovered that we weren't the only ones who were exhausted. When we went downstairs for breakfast, Aunt Holly's door was still closed. She needed a little extra sleep after our nighttime adventure, too.

The breakfast table was once again filled with a variety of food. I noticed the same red jam that was at yesterday's breakfast was on the table again. Brigitta said it was lingonberry jam.

"A what-on-berry?!" I asked.

Aunt Ingrid explained that it grows in Sweden and is a close relative of the cranberry.

I giggled. "Like a cousin?" I asked.

Aunt Ingrid chuckled and said that describing the two similar berries as cousins is a good way of putting it.

"Sometimes people call them 'alpine cranberries,'" she continued.

I decided to try it on a *knackebrod*, which is the Swedish name of a piece of crisp bread, and it was delicious.

All of a sudden an idea popped into my head.

"If they're called 'alpine cranberries' does that mean we can use them in place of cranberries to string with our popcorn for the Christmas tree?" I asked.

"Most certainly," Aunt Ingrid replied.

"Tomorrow we'll string them and put the finishing touches on the tree," Brigitta reminded us. "But the Snowflake Ball is *tonight*, and we have lots of things to do *today*!"

We needed to make sure that we had our handmade snowflakes finished and ready to enter into the Snowflake Ball contest.

Mine was wrapped up in tissue paper and ready to go. Brigitta had worked on several snowflakes and she had to decide which one to enter into the contest.

We asked Hans if he wanted to join us with our last minute details in preparation for the ball. In his somewhat standoffish* manner he said his snowflake was complete and he had taken care of everything.

Brigitta narrowed down her selection and decided to bring the snowflake she had spent the most time on, which was a very fancy one.

She called it "The Newborn Snowflake." Using cotton balls and shiny blue paper, she had created what appeared to be a big cloud with water droplets inside.

Underneath hung a baby snowflake wrapped in a blanket. Attached was a "birth certificate" explaining where the snowflake came from and how it was formed.

I was amazed at how much Brigitta and Hans knew. They really loved to learn and discover new things. They made everything interesting, and it sure made it fun for me!

❧ ☙

In the afternoon, Mom and Aunt Ingrid took Brigitta and me for a quick ride to the downtown open-air market. I wore my quilted vest over a striped shirt. With my snow pants and winter boots, I was toasty warm.

Once we arrived, we stepped out of our car to walk in the cool, crisp outdoor air. We glimpsed twinkling lights and heard carolers singing in the distance.

As we got closer to the market the smell of baked apple strudel and other scrumptious sweets flowed all around us.

"Mmmmmm...." I said, breathing in deeply.

All of these wonderful things hit me with a huge tingle of Christmas spirit!

Aunt Ingrid and Brigitta went one way and my mom and I headed in a different direction so my mom could get some last-minute presents and keep them as a surprise.

As we strolled* among rows of little lighted huts with loads of interesting objects for sale, snowflakes started to fall.

It felt good to be there because it reminded me of Christkindlmarket in Chicago, where we go every holiday season.

This is the perfect place to find perfect gifts! I thought.

People gathered around a hut where a man

was selling brightly painted Dala horses, like the ones Brigitta collected. I asked my mom if I could buy three, each in a different color. I knew they would be great souvenirs* from Sweden to bring back to Caroline, Jenny and Megan.

At another hut we spotted the cutest ornament carved from wood into the shape of a bunny. I don't think we could have ever found a better gift for Caroline to thank her for taking such good care of Mr. Snuggles!

Back at the house we realized it was time to pick out the outfits we would be wearing to the Snowflake Ball.

Brigitta opened the doors to her wardrobe, which had a closet space with shelves, a mirror and a drawer, all in one. Hanging inside were two beautiful dresses. One stood out. It was a long white satin dress with a red sash.

I wondered if she ever wore it. She said she had just worn it last week on Saint Lucia's

Day, which is on the thirteenth of December each year.

"Legend says it is the longest night of the year in Sweden and the day that the Christmas season really begins," she explained.

To celebrate this day, the oldest daughter, a Lucia, wears a long white dress with a red sash, just like Brigitta's. She also wears a crown made of evergreens or twigs, lit with seven battery-operated candles.

She brings coffee, ginger biscuits and special buns called "Lucia cats" to her parents and younger brothers and sisters while they are still in bed.

"That sounds fun," I said. "I wonder why we don't have anything like that in America."

Brigitta brought out her other dress, which was shimmering gold with ruffles along the hem, and a fuchsia-pink satin jacket. Perfect for the holiday!

What will I wear? I thought. I had only packed one special dress that my mom and I had picked out for Christmas Eve.

I mentioned to Brigitta that I wasn't sure if my mom would think it was all right to wear it twice—on Christmas Eve *and* to the ball.

I couldn't ask her right away because Mom was helping with the decorating for the Snowflake Ball and probably wouldn't be back for a while.

When I showed my red dress with layers of ruffles all around the bottom to Brigitta she immediately said, "Wow, that is one of the prettiest dresses I have ever seen!"

She paused for a few seconds.

"Hmm, we really need to find out if your mom will think it's OK to wear it before Christmas Eve."

All of a sudden she had an idea.

"We've got to ask Mormor what she thinks! She'll probably know exactly what your mom will say."

"Brilliant idea, Brigitta!" I exclaimed.

Both of us bolted downstairs and found

Mormor alone in the kitchen. We explained our problem.

"Do you think my mom would mind if I wore my Christmas Eve dress tonight to the Snowflake Ball?" I asked.

"Well, I don't know why she would have a problem with that. I can't think of any better event to wear it to. It's silly to only wear it once," Mormor said.

Just then my mom walked in the back door and saw us.

"You all look like you're plotting* something—what's up?" she asked.

Chapter Nine

THE SNOWFLAKE BALL

Mormor explained that I wanted to wear my special dress to the Snowflake Ball.

"That certainly makes sense. I can't think of a better event to wear it to," she said smiling.

Mormor, Brigitta and I let out a loud giggle all at once.

"Did I say something wrong?" my mom asked.

"No," I said. "We're laughing because that's almost *exactly* what Mormor said when we asked her what she thought!"

Mom joined in the laughter.

Brigitta and I couldn't wait to try on our dresses. I put my dress on and placed each foot carefully into my shiny red shoes and added a matching headband. And then I twirled around so Brigitta could see.

"You look like someone out of a magazine." She paused and said, "You know what? That's giving me an idea. How about putting on a family fashion show?"

"Wow, what a great idea," I said. "Let's try to round everyone up."

As usual, Hans was in his room, behind a closed door.

Mom, Aunt Ingrid and Aunt Holly were sipping tea and relaxing after their hard work helping to decorate the ballroom.

Dad and Uncle Max were busy in the kitchen. Dad was making his famous candy cane cupcakes for the bake sale at the ball.

Mormor was making a snowflake for the contest. Brigitta gave her the box with all the materials and Mormor went to work on her "happy" snowflake with a big smiling face.

"These past few days we've had together

have been wonderful," said Mormor, "I guess this is a good way to express how I feel."

"Mormor, that's just how we feel. Hans and I are so glad everybody is together for the holidays," said Brigitta.

Hans? Did I hear her correctly? Hans? All Hans does is stay in his room all the time with his door shut. Hans is happy we are all together? I find that hard to believe!

When Hans heard about our fashion show he quickly scampered* downstairs to join the family as we gathered in the living room.

Mormor agreed to be the host of the show. She would describe our outfits just like they do on the fashion runway*.

"We now have the lovely Brigitta entering in her shimmering gold dress," Mormor announced.

Brigitta then strolled into a roomful of applause.

Mormor pointed out the ruffles around the hem of Brigitta's dress, the bright, fuchsia-pink jacket with shiny buttons and her pretty shoes.

Brigitta twirled around and curtsied* to our enthusiastic audience.

"And our second model is Ginger, wearing her fabulous ruffled red dress, matching red shoes and a fancy headband." Mormor continued.

I pranced* around the room and everyone applauded.

Dad said, "Wow, you girls are dressed to the nines."

Brigitta and Hans looked at each other with a confused look on their faces.

"What does that mean?" asked Hans.

"It means you are dressed perfectly," Dad explained.

Uncle Max commented that we could not have found any nicer outfits for the holidays.

Brigitta and I were really having fun hamming* it up while we pretended to be fashion models.

Aunt Ingrid stood up and said "I'm sorry to put an end to such great entertainment but everyone needs to get ready because the Snowflake Ball begins in less than two hours."

Mormor, Brigitta, Hans and I gathered up our snowflakes and scurried to Uncle Max's car for our ride to the Art and Music Center.

We arrived twenty minutes before the festivities* were to begin. This gave us time to walk around the main entrance hall and see the interesting artwork and sculptures made by the students.

As we turned the corner to enter the Snowflake Ball I gasped, and we all stopped.

"Wow, this is unbelievable," Dad said.

In front of us was a winter wonderland that Aunt Ingrid, Aunt Holly and my mom had helped create.

A long wall had been painted with a

winter sledding scene that looked real. We were very surprised to hear that Aunt Ingrid had painted it. She said it is called a "mural."

Christmas trees, frosted in fake snow, were placed throughout the hall. Hung from the ceiling among strands of tiny white lights, snowflakes sparkled and silver foil icicles glistened.

We posed in front of the mural as a photographer snapped several photos of us.

People wandered around the room, going from table to table with holiday greetings. Everyone was dressed to the nines, as my dad would say! I was so glad I had gotten to wear my special holiday dress and take part in this magical family tradition.

Snow-white tablecloths covered the tables. Each had a gingerbread house in the center, decorated with white frosting and enough gumdrops and licorice sticks to fill a candy shop!

Lines of people gathered at the back of the

room to dip their cups into big bowls of bright red holiday punch. Large platters of fresh fruit and appetizers spilled onto the long tables.

As we continued to stroll about, a children's choir stood on the stage. Their soft voices soothed us as they sang Christmas carols.

We got so distracted* by everything that we almost forgot to place our snowflakes on the display tables.

More than a hundred snowflakes were entered into the contest. Some were made of paper. Many were made of recycled materials like shiny buttons, bits of fabric and old polished hardware.

We noticed the judges slowly walking around with clipboards, observing each snowflake carefully. They looked very serious.

Our plates were heaped with a variety of salads, fresh breads, delicious vegetable and fruit spreads and every kind of holiday food you could imagine.

The room was filled with anticipation

as everyone waited for the snowflake award ceremony to begin.

At last the judges began to announce all the special categories starting with "most festive." After a few minutes they moved on to the "most interesting facts" category. The head judge gave the award for honorable mention and then she announced, "Our first place prize goes to Brigitta!"

"Hooray!" we whooped, while jumping up and down and hugging each other.

Many more winners were announced.

Soon one of the judges said it was time to present the "most beautiful snowflake" award.

"And the winner is…." He paused, and then said loudly, "Hans…for his "Cousin Ginger Snowflake."

For a split second I thought it must be a joke. All I could do was sit there in disbelief with my mouth wide open!

Chapter Ten

HOLIDAY MAGIC

After all the awards were given out, we went up to the front of the ballroom where all the winners were displayed. There was the "Cousin Ginger Snowflake" with its big red first place ribbon.

"Isn't it lovely?" Mormor asked, as I carefully picked it up for a closer look.

Hans was explaining to us how he came up with the idea. After Brigitta and I had made our first batch of cookies that was such a disaster, Hans was worried the dough was going to be thrown out.

"You both put so much work into that batch of cookies and I didn't want to see it go to waste."

He described how he had used cookie

cutters and small tools to shape it into a very fancy design. He added some old, broken costume* jewelry to give it sparkle, and let the dough harden.

As I gazed* at the gorgeous snowflake, I couldn't believe my eyes. My cousin Hans, who I thought didn't like me very much, had made the most spectacular snowflake *in the whole wide world* and named it after *me*!

I never pictured myself wrapping my arms around Hans to give him a big hug but that was just what I did—right in the middle of the Snowflake Ball!

Cഈ Cഈ

The more I thought about everything the following morning, the more I realized that I had been wrong to feel uncomfortable about Hans. I looked at him in an entirely different way. No longer did I see him as the cousin who didn't want me there.

Just as I walked out into the hallway,

Aunt Holly was leaving her room.

"Ginger, are you ready to put all the final decorations on the tree today?" she asked.

"You bet I am," I said.

This was the day to hang my glittering pink ball ornament with the striped ribbon from Mormor. It was the day to string popcorn and lingonberries. And it was the day to find a special place for "Nutmeg Gnome" on the tree.

We went to the kitchen to get some breakfast. Hans was sitting at the table.

"Hans, what a nice surprise! What are you doing here?" asked Aunt Holly.

"I'm just about finished with all my projects so I figured I'd have breakfast with you," he said.

I wondered what kind of projects he was referring to. *Do they give out so much homework in Sweden that he has to spend his holiday time working?*

Oh well, at least he wasn't ignoring us and he was actually eating breakfast with us.

This is a first! I thought.

Mom, Dad, Aunt Ingrid and Uncle Max were busy getting the food ready. Mormor loves to bake, so she had all the ingredients spread out to make mouthwatering cookies, just like at home.

"We can't make our popcorn garlands without a cup of hot chocolate," Aunt Holly said, looking at me with a big smile. She handed me a glass mug with pink and red hearts on it, full of delicious hot chocolate.

After we finished breakfast, we gathered the popcorn and berries and began stringing them. I was surprised how quickly Hans joined in. He was having a hard time threading his needle so I showed him how to do it.

Shortly after we started, Brigitta appeared.

"It sure does smell good in here," she said as she pulled up a chair and began eating her usual open-faced sandwich for breakfast. When she finished, she enthusiastically started stringing the garlands.

All of a sudden I noticed something. I stood up and said, "Do you see what I see?"

We rushed to the window and gazed out at freshly falling snow. Aunt Holly described it as "enchanting."

"Maybe it will be a white Christmas after all, just like in Chicago," I said.

What fun! I thought. *It's as if someone waved a magical holiday wand over me!*

Chapter Eleven

THE CHRISTMAS EVE VISITOR

"Hans, it's cold outside. Why are you putting your shoes out there on the doorstep?" I asked, while trying not to laugh.

"Because it is a custom in Sweden to put shoes out on Christmas Eve. We always put ours outside on the doorstep. Last Christmas I found money and some small gifts in my shoes!" he answered excitedly.

"Everyone opens gifts on the night before Christmas in Sweden. An old legend is that *Jultomten*, a white-bearded gnome, brings gifts to the door on Christmas Eve. He is thought to live in the attic or under the floor in a home or a barn. Some think he lives in the forest," he said.

Hans continued telling me all about

Jultomten. He comes carrying a huge sack, loaded with presents, on his back. The gifts are wrapped in brightly colored Christmas paper with amusing poems that give hints about what's inside the boxes.

After he told me this I was so excited. I could hardly wait until evening in hopes of a visit from *Jultomten.*

❧ ☙

Uncle Max and Aunt Ingrid knew we would all enjoy a Christmas Eve smorgasbord.

"The three of you can help get it ready," said Uncle Max.

Brigitta explained that a smorgasbord is a table full of a variety of foods.

Our smorgasbord included things I had never seen before, like pickled beets. There was an onion-and-potato casserole baking, and boy, did that smell delicious!

"Wow, I've never eaten anything like this," I said.

"Here, try some pickled beets," coaxed Brigitta, as she began spooning some onto a plate for me.

After she handed it to me I poked a fork into one of the slices.

"It smells like a pickle," I commented. And then I popped the entire huge, juicy beet slice into my mouth.

Brigitta started to giggle.

"What's the matter?" I asked.

"You have big purplish-red lips," she laughed, as she pulled me over to a mirror to see.

We both began to cackle* hysterically.

"Where did Hans go?" I asked, as I tried to stop giggling. "He's got to see this!"

Just then Hans walked in from the living room.

"I leave the room for one minute and you two have a giggle party!" he said smiling.

He then turned his head to look at me and let out a huge laugh.

"Golly, Ginger what did you do, stick your mouth in the bowl of pickled beets?"

"No, but I think I'll have a few more if it's OK," I replied.

"Sounds like a good idea," said Brigitta.

We all decided to sit down and enjoy a helping.

Since I love pickles, I enjoyed the beets. Not only did they taste good, it was fun to see

88

what purple beet juice would do to our lips and tongues!

ᕙ ᕗ

We arranged the table for Christmas Eve and helped set out the food for the smorgasboard. Even though some of it tasted funny to me, it was interesting to try new and unusual things.

The cinnamon aroma of *risgrynsgrot* simmering on the stove flowed throughout the house. *Risgrynsgrot* was one thing I really enjoyed trying. It's a sweet, creamy rice porridge with one almond hidden in it. The person who finds the almond gets to make a wish.

I was so happy when I found the almond in my porridge. Since I never got my wish when we cracked our ginger cookies I now had a second chance to make up for it!

We were all chatting away while finishing our desserts. Suddenly, I jumped from my seat, startled to hear a loud knock on the door. Aunt

Ingrid hopped up to see who it was.

When she opened the door it was *Jultomten*. He yelled out, "Are there any good children here?" And then he tossed some boxes inside and ran away.

"My, my, look what we have here," said Aunt Ingrid smiling.

He had left three boxes, which were all the same size. Each box was beautifully wrapped with a shiny red satin bow. One gift had a card on it for "Brigitta," one for "Hans" and one for "Ginger." Aunt Ingrid explained that each Christmas present was called a *julklapp* or Christmas box.

Aunt Ingrid handed me my box. I noticed there was something written on it and I began to read the words:

Take a journey along a trail
and float above the snow.
You're sure to glide and even sail
while traveling to and fro.

"Hmm," I said.

And then Hans was given his box and read the note:

Tracks in the snow are fun to see
with every step you take.
You'll stride among the fresh snowfall
and welcome each snowflake.

"I wonder what it is," he said, shaking it.

Next it was Brigitta's turn. She looked at me, and almost in a whisper, asked, "What in the world?" And then she read the message on her gift:

You'll stay dry with every step,
no soggy socks or feet.
Put these on and go outside
for a walk that's a special treat.

We all looked at one another with a big smile. With the speed of light, each of us ripped the wrapping paper off our gifts, and to our surprise we had each received our own pair of snowshoes.

I squealed with excitement when I saw my beautiful pink snowshoes with striped straps.

Brigitta and Hans jumped up and down.

Mormor suggested that we try them out immediately. With our parents' approval, we ran upstairs to change out of our dressy outfits.

While I threw on my quilted vest, snow pants, boots and ski goggles, Brigitta quickly pulled on her coat and grabbed earmuffs, mittens and boots, stopping only to help Hans find his snow pants.

We all ran outside and scrambled to put our snowshoes on. They attached right to our boots with the bindings. It was a race to see who could make the first snowshoe print in the fresh fallen snow!

Snowshoeing is a great way to walk on deep snow without sinking. With a little bit of practice we soon got the hang of it. For more than an hour, we played outdoors wearing our snowshoes. I don't think I've ever had so much fun!

It was such an adventure to follow animal tracks in the snow by the light of the moon.

"Look over there!" I pointed. "Those tracks look like they were made by Mr. Snuggles!"

I followed the tracks with my eyes. In the snow, with whiskers twitching, was an adorable little brown bunny.

Brigitta and Hans ran over to the spot and the bunny quickly hopped away.

"Is that someone's pet rabbit?" I asked in a worried voice.

"Oh no, that's Little Bernie," Brigitta told me. "We think that's the wild bunny that hops across our yard every night."

"C'mon!" Hans exclaimed. "Let's go make our own tracks."

As we glided and shuffled along, we twisted around to see what kinds of tracks we had made. Then we clomped down real hard to see how our tracks could change. It's a night I'll always remember.

Chapter Twelve

GINGER'S WISH

We didn't open all our presents on Christmas Eve. After all, this was a Swedish-American Christmas, so we saved some presents for Christmas day. We wanted to follow our American tradition, too.

I had brought some special gifts from home for Brigitta and Hans. On Christmas morning, I was just about ready to hand them out when Hans gave me the most beautifully decorated box with a glittery silver bow. There was something written on it:

Something is inside
that's easy to chew,
but it's not for a human
so I'll give you a clue.

When I opened it up I was surprised to see another wrapped box nested inside with a second poem attached:

It's made from a willow tree
filled with dry hay,
and some twigs to munch
with some toys for play.

If you guessed a basket
you would be right,
since it's for a little guy
who is black and white.

Cheers to Mr. Snuggles,
he's such a lucky boy
to have the best friend in the whole wide world,
The Great Ginger from Chicago, Illinois!

Inside the box was a woven-willow basket lined with hay. It was filled to the top with rabbit toys and dried fruit treats.

There is a Swedish tradition to put out a sheaf* of wheat on Christmas Eve for the animals, so Hans had placed one in the basket for Mr. Snuggles. He had even fashioned each letter of Mr. Snuggles' name from apple tree twigs, which rabbits like to chew.

Then Brigitta handed me another box, wrapped in shiny silver-and-pink paper and tied with a sparkly bow. I excitedly read the poem that was on the card:

We didn't know how we'd feel
about your visit here.
We were a bit nervous
with a touch of fear.

Our wish was that you'd like us
and you'd feel right at home.
We placed our baskets on the tree
along with "Nutmeg Gnome."

Until there is another time
that we can be together,
we'll crack our cookies and make a wish
for our memories to last forever!

I opened the gift and inside was a heart basket that held handmade straw ornaments.

Separately wrapped in tissue paper were a heart and letters, made from twigs, that spelled out G-I-N-G-E-R.

"Wow, these are awesome!" I exclaimed.

"I collected twigs and made them myself," Hans said proudly.

"Oh Hans, you put so much time and imagination into these presents," I said, "and you're *so* thoughtful."

So that's it! Now I get it, I said to myself. *The reason Hans always shut his door and acted like he wanted to be alone was because he was busy making special gifts for Mr. Snuggles and me.*

With a big smile on my face, I handed my presents to Hans and Brigitta.

I gave them each a stocking that I had helped embroider with their names. They were filled with holiday treats like ribbon candy and red-and-white peppermint candy canes.

I had picked out a bright blue scarf as a gift for Hans.

And for Brigitta, I had brought a snow globe with a scene of winter in Chicago.

When it was my turn to open up her gift to me I was so surprised to find it was also a snow globe—of *Jultomten*!

Brigitta stood up and declared, "I am so happy that the wish I made while cracking my

cookie has come true. My wish was for Ginger to become my close friend."

"And that's almost the exact thing I wished for!" I chimed in. "But there was one other thing, and that was for Hans to be my close friend, too."

The best Christmas present I received was the gift of friendship with my newfound cousins.

I never thought I would want to put off packing for our trip home. And I never thought the day would come when I really wouldn't want to leave.

It was almost like having a home away from home! This Christmas was the best Christmas *in the whole wide world*!

Power of a Girl Initiative

For every Our Generation doll, outfit or accessory you buy, a portion of sales goes to Free The Children's Power of a Girl Initiative to help provide girls in developing countries an education—the most powerful tool in the world for escaping poverty.

Did you know that out of the millions of children who aren't in school, 70% of them are girls? In developing communities around the world, many girls can't go to school. Usually it's because there's no school available or because their responsibilities to family (farming, earning an income, walking hours each day for water) prevent it.

Free The Children has now built more than 650 schools which educate more than 55,000 children throughout the developing world. Free The Children also builds and fosters sustainable villages through healthcare, water programs and alternate income projects for moms and dads that give girls the opportunity to get the education they need.

The most incredible part is that most of Free The Children's funding comes from kids just like you, holding lemonade stands, bake sales, penny drives, walkathons and more.

Just by buying an Our Generation doll or accessory you have helped change the world, and you are powerful (beyond belief!) to help even more.

If you want to find out more, visit:
www.ogdolls.com/free-the-children

FREE THE CHILDREN
children helping children through education

Free The Children provided the factual information pertaining to their organization.
Free The Children is a 501c3 organization.

Ginger's Holiday Adventure

Ginger's travels were full of wonderful holiday fun,
traditions and surprises! Now here's some fun for you—
a list of hidden words from Ginger's adventure is below.
Make a copy of the next page. Then find and circle the
words from the list that are hidden in the grid.
Here's a hint: the words go up, down, forward, backward
and diagonal (from one corner to the other)!
The solution is on page 107 (at the end of the Glossary).
No peeking yet ☺

COUSINS
HANS
BRIGITTA
DALA
HOLIDAY
LINGONBERRY
SNOWFLAKES
WISHES
COCKADOODLEDOO
GNOME
JULTOMTEN
PEPPARKAKOR
SNOWSHOES
KNACKEBROD
RISGRYNSGROT
SWEDEN

Word Search

S	L	T	N	J	H	U	S	A	X	S	J	S	P	R
W	A	I	E	E	G	O	T	S	N	F	O	E	O	I
E	L	G	N	L	T	T	L	O	N	E	M	O	N	S
D	A	R	O	G	I	M	W	I	I	A	D	H	B	G
E	D	H	I	G	O	F	O	J	D	E	H	S	F	R
N	N	U	I	P	L	N	Y	T	L	A	G	W	T	Y
V	H	R	J	A	W	Q	B	D	L	O	Y	O	Y	N
W	B	W	K	I	T	W	O	E	Z	U	D	N	L	S
Q	P	E	S	Z	Z	O	Y	B	R	U	J	S	J	G
T	S	H	A	W	D	R	O	R	W	R	A	U	H	R
P	E	P	P	A	R	K	A	K	O	R	Y	J	Q	O
S	Q	U	K	C	O	U	S	I	N	S	X	D	C	T
Y	C	C	F	U	J	Y	O	M	D	Y	A	W	A	Q
X	O	D	O	R	B	E	K	C	A	N	K	P	A	J
C	A	S	L	A	K	U	V	G	N	O	M	E	B	B

103

Glossary

*Many words have more than one meaning. Here are the definitions of words marked with this symbol ******* (an asterisk) as they are used in sentences.*

abandoning: *leaving something behind
    with no plan to return*
ambitious: *wanting to do great things*
ancestors: *people who were in your
    family a very long time ago*
anxious: *uneasy and worried*
blue: *sad*
broached, as in "broached the subject":
    brought up
bungalow: *a type of house with one
    floor and a low roof*
bustling: *busy*
cackle: *noisy laugh*
citizen: *a person who lives in a city*
coincidental: *when two or more things
    happen at the same time*
costume, as in "costume jewelry":
    not made of real gold or gems

curtsied: *bowed down by bending the knees with one foot forward*

distracted: *unable to pay attention*

embroider: *decorate cloth with a needle and thread*

enthusiastically: *excitedly*

festive: *merry*

festivities: *celebrations with lots of activities*

frustration: *a feeling of irritation and helplessness*

gazed: *looked thoughtfully*

generation: *the period of time between the birth of parents and the birth of their children*

hamming, as in "hamming it up": *purposely acting in an exaggerated way*

immigrated: *came to a new country to live*

index, as in "index finger": *pointer finger*

mementos: *items that remind a person of something*

panicked: *felt full of fear*

plotting: *secretly planning something*

pranced: *walked in a lively way*

reminiscing: *remembering things from the past*

reputation: *what people think about a person*

resented: *felt anger about something*

retreated: *backed away*

runway: *what models walk along in fashion shows*

scampered: *ran*

sheaf: *a bundle of wheat or other grain plants tied together*

shelter, as in "animal shelter": *a place where people help and protect homeless animals, including lost pets*

souvenirs: *items kept as reminders of a place that was visited*

standoffish: *unfriendly*

strolled: *walked slowly*

T, as in "to a T": *exactly right*

tradition: *an event that has been done for a long time and becomes the usual thing to do*

trait: *a special quality that makes a person different*

unison: *all together or at the same time*

Word Search Solution

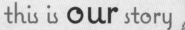

this is **our** story

We are an extraordinary generation of girls. And have we got a story to tell.

Our Generation is unlike any that has come before. We're helping our families learn to recycle, holding bake sales to support charities, and holding penny drives to build homes for orphaned children in Haiti. We're helping our little sisters learn to read and even making sure the new kid at school has a place to sit in the cafeteria.

All that and we still find time to play hopscotch and hockey. To climb trees, do cartwheels all the way down the block and laugh with our friends until milk comes out of our noses. You know, to be kids.

Will we have a big impact on the world? We already have. What's ahead for us? What's ahead for the world? We have no idea. We're too busy grabbing and holding on to the joy that is today.

Yep. This is our time. This is our story.

www.ogdolls.com

About the Author

Cynthia (Cindy) Haigh, a mother and grandmother, lives in the Boston area. From the time she was a little girl she has cared deeply about animals and has been very involved with several animal protection groups. It was always difficult for her to hear all the stories of animals without homes, and over the years she and her family ended up adopting dozens of animals, from cats to rabbits. In fact, one of her rabbits, Little Bob, provided the inspiration for Ginger's rabbit, Mr. Snuggles.

She presently has two dogs, Petey and Larry, who were adopted from animal shelters. Thanks to them making friends with a teensy-weensy dog named Louie, also adopted from an animal shelter, she would go on walks with Louie's human buddy, Maggie, who grew up in Sweden. Some of Maggie's memories of her life in Sweden became part of Ginger's story.

This story also came to life because of all the wonderful people who contributed their creativity and vision, including Joe Battat, Dany Battat, Loredana Ramacieri, Karen Erlichman, Sandy Jacinto, Véronique Casavant, Véronique Chartrand, Jenny Gambino, Natalie Cohen, Lisa Armstrong, Joanne Burke Casey and Pam Shrimpton. Many thanks to Gisela Voss for the wonderfully creative concept she came up with.

In addition to **Home Away from Home,** *Cindy has written several other children's books including* **The Marvelous Math Book, Hoppin' Healthy Harvesters, Busy Beaver Launderette, Sweep, Mop, Sparkle and Shine Specialists** *and she co-authored* **Bugz Bugz. . .What's the buzz about bugs?**

this is my holiday story:

this is my wish list: